Billy Olive
"UNDEFEATED"

Billy Olive
"UNDEFEATED"

3,000 Heists Across America

J. BANNER JOHNSON

Contents

BILLY "O" AND THE ROOFTOPPERS

B y now they had their "dance of the night" down to perfection. Billy Olive would always travel to an obscure town or city two or three days ahead of the rest of his band. He dressed appropriately for the times, a not too fanciful suit and tie, often bringing a suitcase to appear as a lawyer or business consultant. After a day or two of learning the habits of the people in town, Billy Olive would sit on the couch or chair in the front window of his modest hotel room across the street from the location of the band's gig. He could see the people's comings and goings, day for night, while they, the crowd, could not make the same claim.

Sometime on the third day of the journey, four other members of the band arrived in town to meet Billy Olive, and rehearse the music he created from the sights and sounds of the city. One of his mates was a master at listening for the ever so silent humming of wires. Another, was a percussion man, with a keen ear for the odd sounds of certain clicks and clacks. The third member of the band was a cool, calm and collective gentleman, with an eye of an eagle, spotting any-thing that moved or seemed to be out of place; And then there was Billy Olive. When they were on, and they were "on" every weekend for forty years, they made beautiful music together.

The national retail store that carried a top line of men's suits was located across from Billy Olive's suite, in a brand-new shopping mall. He and his band mates would need to be properly outfitted, with new suits, ties and shoes, for the highly anticipated evening. His band members, having settled into their rooms with differing views of the shopping mall and the side maintenance walkways, were warming up for the night's events. Maids and butlers working in the modest hotel in town would later describe hearing a radio or television play-ing a song or a television show most of the night, the music blaring from the four rooms rented by the out of towners. Late in the night, around 2:00 a.m., Billy Olive would be the first band member to enter the location of the gig. He preferred going through the back door. If locked, the special skills of one of his fellow band members made this only a trifling complication. The band had a show to put on, a job to do, and they were entering the theatre to prepare, no matter what.

The crew was now together, and more importantly, the fans, al-though unusually quiet, came to see their act. Although there were four hundred well maintained suits standing up in the crowd, no one was in them. The band, taking notice of this unusual circumstance, still appreciated their attendance as they loaded all four hundred of them into a large tractor-trailer container truck, sitting idle, en-gine on, ten feet from the backdoor of the theatre. One of the band members, it was later surmised, went back inside to chat with four fans sitting near the front window, above the floor and on a wooden platform, just inches from the pane glass windows of this magnifi-cent looking palace. In a gesture that would prove noteworthy later, the lead guitarists would remove the suits, shirts, ties, pants, socks, shoes and hats from the storefront fans, as he dashed back to the sixteen-wheeler, clothes and apparel in tow.

Thirty minutes later, the band was done for the evening. The town police had not noticed their performance until they were long gone. It was not until two uniforms, in a black and white vehicle, conducting a routine patrol around the front of the mall's anchor store, observed what was later described as an "unusual site." Four storefront mannequins were sitting naked at a table, in all their glory, giving the patrolmen their first hint that something was afoot. Later, during a very, very brief news conference, the town's chief of police concluded that a prestigious men's store, the pride of Newfoundland Falls, had been stripped of every piece of clothing and apparel not nailed down to the floor. The naked mannequins themselves attended this public announcement and confirmed, by their mere shameless presence, what the chief had stated.

The debut of Billy Olive's band was indeed a show stopper. News of their professional work travelled five states ahead of them, transforming the crew into some sort of phenomena. For Billy and his band, this night would be a perfect heist in what would be the beginning of their magnificent season.

THE INTERSECTION OF WOOD AND QUISNER

"Is it open for lunch?"

"I think it is, today."

"What time do they.."

"When the whistle blows, and it rumbles home; The 5:15."

It was the hottest day of the year.

Chapter I

LOWELLVILLE

William George Olive would come out screaming in the bucolic town of Lowellville, Ohio, sometime in the month of August, 1930. He would grow up in a pre-dominately Italian community, working the family business, (a gutter and roof repair business), with his grandfather, the legendary Pop Shraum, his father Dominic, by each account a saint, his loving and tender mother Vivian and two jumping sisters, Shirley (Pinky) Olive and JoAnne (Bunny) Olive. They would live near mystical railroad tracks, where church bells were rung by angels, alongside the mighty, muddy, Mahoning River. Acres of green pasture and farmland fed the men who brewed the mysterious iron ore recipe that made the steel that built this country. They lived in surrounding homes constructed by settlers before the civil war. The waters of the Mahoning came out of the ground near the confluence of the three rivers in nearby Pittsburgh, Pennsylvania. The cold, cool streams of the rumbling Mahoning helped quench the hot metal produced by the gigantic steel mills in nearby Youngstown, Ohio. This was America, with all its harnessed sweat and beauty, the bulk of which was waiting to be unleashed to fight worlds of wars and create a nation of opportunity. It was Norman Rockwell on steroids, and much, much more.

Young William "Billy" Olive, working with his father and grandfather, sprouted up in that jazy little town. The three of them, while young Bill was of school age, put in an honest day's work, fixing gutters, rooftops and barns in and around their hometown of Lowellville. They toiled daily just a click away from the industrial powerhouse of Youngstown, Ohio, "The Steel City". Coming out of the depression and war years, Pop Shraum was the toast of the town. He was like Santa Claus, delivering coal to homes, shooting the charcoal colored orbs down into the historic depression era coal slides, on a weekly schedule. Pops never turned down a soul in need, money be damned. He was a councilman for 29 years in this village of immigrants, running without opposition. He was everyone's grandfather and young William George Olive idolized him. Pops was the man who made the cold of winter flee, its last push of icy crystallized air blowing harmlessly into the skies of the coming spring, ushering in promises of a new beginning. During the cold damp rains of the new season, Pops and his boys kept families dry from the needle like, piercing frigid spring rain that only a northerner can know. The Olive family's roof patches and gutter repairs, some said, were the only thing keeping the local houses standing. At any time of the year, the subtle but unmistakable beautiful noise of Pop's rickety truck rivaled the sound of the chiming savior's bell atop the local church tower. If they could just hold on, stay a little warm by rubbing their cold hands together, or hiding under the dry spots of a soaked blanket, they could survive another day; The warming brightness of summer would then be one instant closer.

Pops would often navigate his wagon of rust over the double railroad tracks that ran through the center of town. These tricky, magical tracks were matched only by their better half, that cool, quiet at times, but fast flowing Mahoning River. "Rush along mighty Mahoning, wave after wave of glittering magic, you hide your place of birth well, but all know where it is that you are carrying your teaming waters too."

The raw, ear shattering whistles of the iron maidens passing through the center of town, were a signal to many to calibrate their silver and gold timepieces worn inside their pockets. Many of them, mostly retired railroad engineers and steel workers, would be drinking Italian coffee (espresso) while arguing the politics of the day, as they dined at the local Iron Man Inn. The squealing wheels of the train, from time to time, would give away a stray animal's location as the iron horse, approaching the middle of town, slowed a bit, giving an extra blast of its whistle to alert wayward farm animals in its path.

These striking sounds of the day set the rhythm of the town and its folk. It was alive with hope and in constant, deliberate motion according to its role assigned by the universe. The village itself was a bill- board for American toughness and sheer will power. Each day the town awoke and smacked down its hard labor, was itself an act of defiance to the axis monsters who sought their demise. Other towns may come and go, but the farmers, steel workers and wives raising the many children of Lowellville, Ohio, would forever be loyal and present when called to stand for that shiney nation on the hill, America.

Chapter II

GROWING UP OLIVE

I t was around 1943, or 1944, during wartime, that Pops, his son
Dominic, (Billy's father), and young Billy Olive were finishing a
week's work at the Carcella property (car-sell-a) on the east end
of town. The family crew was patching leaking gutters at the widow
Carcella's home, so as to stop the flooding of her victory garden
planted in the backyard. Young Bill was helping Pops with a shutter
in the back room, nailing it to the somewhat rotting wood. The trio,
who worked up an appetite for garden greens, tomatoes, chicken
and pasta, were scheduled to be at dinner at their beckoning home,
hidden up in a wooded area, away for the mystical tracks, and resting
above the west branch of the whipping Mahoning. This was Indian
country not long ago, and Bill, as he was heading toward the call of
the 'matron' of the palace, delighted in an arrowhead he had found
at the end of the day's work.

As with every day at this time, another train, proceeding down
one of the two tracks in the center of town, was whistling by, (at 5:15
pm), heading to Youngstown with its payload of the blackest iron

ore and coal unearthed in nearby Pennsylvania and West Virginia. Young Bill, his archeological find in hand, was crossing these tracks and limbering up the hill toward his mother's cooking. His father, back at the "Olive gutter and Rooftop" business office, no doubt heard the steamy scream of the approaching locomotive, considering it as just another reminder that it was quitting time. It was an eerie, but beautiful dusk that day, the sun peeking through the dim, coal dusted air. Yet, a little darkness was welcomed, as it was a sign that people were working and the country and its war effort was moving toward victory.

Young Bill had, on this day as in many prior days, glanced back to look for pops. There was a penalty if you were late. In Lowellville, food was a close second to the love of God. As Bill scouted the tracks near the Iron Man Inn, its patrons and their young grandsons, who were smuggled into that inner sanctum, were taking friendly bets on whether the train whistle was for one, or two trains, the second track only being seldom used. The young children inside this otherworldly Inn were enchanted by the rusted oil burning lamps, stacked in a row up against the dark scarlet wall of the beer garden. The children saw the magic in them, and every secret lantern inside this cave brought their dreams of becoming a railroad engineer closer to reality. But it was wartime, and the future engineers would have to be patient. The steel mills needed all the iron and might to fight the Third Reich, all of it coming courtesy of Lowellville's railroad tracks and the pumping rapids of the river. It seemed at times that these two forces challenged each other in a sprint to the finish line, drawn in white chalk somewhere in the mysterious steel yards a few miles away. Amidst the commotion and noise coming from the Iron Man Inn, young Bill hollered once again for his beloved grandfather, as he was absent from his shoulder's glance. He lost track of Pops as the sun, setting at just the right angle and amazingly large and low in the summer sky, blinded him.

Some would later say, when questioned by railroad investigators, that they heard the sound of a second whistle, a warning of a second train to come, rambling with great speed and quickness, travelling close behind the 5:15. It was indeed an easy sport to pass in front of the first iron horse, when it ran alone. In fact, the conductors were used to it, although they did not favor the folly of youth. But that day, the second, twin train, shielded by the black sun and the steaming 5:15, was close behind. Suddenly and without warning, a gut wrenching thump, and moaning of a certain kind, was heard coming from the tracks. Men, stumbling and falling over themselves as they poured out of the rustic Iron Man Inn, gathered to witness the commotion birthing near the track. As these men began to heed, the first thought was of a stray animal that perhaps was struck by the 5:15, despite the warning of a whistle. It was not unusual for the local farmers to pick over the fresh carcass of a cow or pig that fell victim to the speeding iron carriage. But the growing laments of the tavern patrons suggested something of a more serious nature had occurred.

Young William, with only the fleeting thought of circling back to gather Papa Shraum for dinner, took a few slow, hesitant steps back down the hill, his eyes locked onto that certain gathering site on the track. Later in life, an older Bill recalled that he clearly remembered shuffling slowly, with a frightened pause, along the trackside gravel, running toward the crowd of men- leading to the point of interest. Young William saw one, then two heads turn. Mr. Antonucci and his relative, visiting from his home village in Southern Italy, locked eyes with him. Young Bill's ankles buckled quickly as he looked down at the object of the men's focus. He stared at the figure, lying motionless on the track, with fixed eyes glancing back at him. Pop Shraum lay dead upon the tracks, his arms wide open over the rails, reminiscent of the man in a painting which hung from a cracked, dark greenish wall in the cold basement of the Iron Man Inn.

Young Bill, upon looking at the face of this beloved grandfather, took flight. Many of the town folk swear he began running, like a frightened, wild rabbit, strangely similar to the ones he used to trap, trying to escape the reality of it all. He ran up the hill and toward his mother's kitchen, then back down toward his father's gutter and roof repair barn, last seen disappearing into the wooded jungle behind the farm of Stephano Berarducci. Chickens and other fowl could be heard cackling, sounding the only alarm nature had given them, announcing that something was very much wrong. A young school teacher later passed down her haunting, but crystal-clear recollection held for years, of a young Bill running for hours, in medical shock, unable to speak or gain a sense of his whereabouts or his very name. After a time, he shuffled back home, to his father and mother, who had half the town looking for him. The next day, they took hold of his young hand, looked into his lost eyes, and slowly walked young William toward the home of the village's undertaker. It wasn't until sometime later that he understood that one of the few pure things in life, and his only reference point for existence, was now gone.

Grandpa Shraum was committed to the grounds of the village cemetery, which took in its children at a place high atop the village below. Hundreds of people gathered as the guilt stricken whistle of the train wailed out its haunting dirge, and the slushing, rambling waters of the mighty Mahoning passed quietly by to pay its respects. Bill spent the better part of the time, staring at the hills and green pastures of his hometown, cursing at the sound of the whistle of the evening train.

When the town was tucked in and asleep that night, a crashing sound could be heard, coming from the direction of the railroad tracks. Young Bill was missing from his cloth bed. As the widow Scaramouch looked toward the dimly lit light near the Iron Man Inn, she could see the figure of a slender tall boy. She recalled glimpses of a stick of some sort, whipping around, crashing, crushing and finally demolishing the railroad warning lights and bells standing at attention next to the mystical tracks. Someone was punishing them for not preventing a catastrophe that would shape a young boy's life. One newcomer suggested he be reported to the town's police chief. That suggestion disappeared as quickly as the morning mist, hovering over the Mahoning, was burned away by the rising sun. Pop Shraum was gone, and Bill learned the first lesson of his life; Nothing lasts forever.

Chapter III

BASEBALL AND OTHER THINGS

The official graduating class yearbook of Lowellville High School, published in 1947, contained printed comments, predictions and aspirations written by the students themselves. The Great War was over, and the whole world was now for the taking by these young spirited souls.

Billy Olive was a natural athlete. After being a quiet but somewhat mischievous student in the local halls of learning, the citizens of Lowellville soon learned they had a bona fide athletic prospect in their midst. William "Billy" Olive, man about town, excelled in Football, Basketball, Volleyball, Track and in his most beloved sport, Baseball. But it was Baseball that claimed him. It was always Baseball. This was America and it could not be any other way.

Billy was a left-handed curveball pitcher, and could hit with the best of them. At fourteen years old, young Bill was playing in the Lawrence County Baseball league. When Billy started for the

Lackawanna Aces, the skinny kid from Lowellville was tossing no-hitters against men twice his age, some being former major league players. His legend was born as his Class B and semi-professional teams began to win championships on the strength and guile of his left arm. Billy's long angular hook, when combined with his tall, lanky build and extended, elongated legs, turned him into an unhittable pitching machine. He was, in a word, perfect. Billy Olive's name was perched on the lips of every major league scout in the area. He was becoming a local legend and on schedule for the "Big Show," the majors.

But with Billy Olive, those crazy, twisting, unhittable dropping curveballs, were only part of the package. His long angular arms and powerful wrists fueled a wickedly powerful left-handed swing. Billy Olive would routinely hit .350 in the very seasons he posted records for pitching performances. But deep down, among all the chatter and fanfare, Billy Olive's biggest thrill was knowing his father and sisters, Bunny and Pinky, were following his every move. They attended his greatest games and became permanent historians of the kid who became a local hero in a game that inspired a nation.

Months after Billy Olive graduated from the relatively unknown haunts of Lowellville High School, he, along with Benny, his partner in crime, packed up the car and drove directly to Southern Florida, admiring their first sighting of palm trees somewhere at the end of Georgia and the beginning of Northern Florida. The New York Giants were conducting 'walk-on' tryouts in the late spring of 1948. As only in a dream, Billy Olive's heroes were there; Hall of Fame legends, Mel Ott, one of the most powerful hitters of all time, two notches down from the Babe himself, and Carl Hubbell, the Hall of Fame pitcher who, to this day, is considered by many as one of the top ten pitchers who ever played the game. Now here comes Billy Olive. The legends watch him display his talents. In this world, these crossing of paths are a thing of destiny. They are ordained, as they are beyond any logical happenstance. It was during this meeting of fate and destiny, that his flashes of brilliance captured their immediate attention.

Billy Olive, fresh off the farm in Lowellville, Ohio, was offered a contract to play Major League Baseball, at $150.00 a month. But after considering his many options, and there were none, Billy relied on the advice of his fellow teenage traveler and turned down the offer to play Major League Baseball. "Go back home and play more AA ball, Billy." "You watch, they will offer you more next year." Billy Olive, all of eighteen years old, and now with a "super-agent" calling his shots, returned to the sandlots of Youngstown, Ohio. That same year, in a late summer game he played at Perkins Park in nearby Warren, Ohio, Billy wound up with a high leg kick, releasing his long left arm, whipping it around like a sea monster popping out of the depths of the ocean, launching the ball toward the catcher's dusty mitt. The crowd cheered, then abruptly stopped. Attached to the echo of these cheers, baseball fans could detect the distinct sound of a quick shoulder pop. The silence grew. Billy later walked off the field and left the game. He could no longer pitch that day, or for that matter, for the balance of that season. Young Billy was badly injured. His left arm was now made of jelly, and soon he was gone from the game. It almost seemed un-American. At eighteen, Billy Olive had lost the second love of his life, Baseball.

"Where have you gone, Joe DiMaggio? A nation turns its lonely eyes to you, wo wo wo What's that you say, Mrs. Robinson 'Joltin Joe' has left and gone away, hey hey hey Hey hey hey.." (Paul Simon).

Chapter IV

"PINKY"

Billy Olive had a little sister named Shirley, who was nicknamed "Pinky" by her neighbor, Mrs. Leonelli. She was that little hustle and bustle who ran around the neighborhood doing all sorts of childish things in the late 1940's. Billy was older and following his own life's path, but Pinky was dancing away, the mad little dancer pinky, twirling around the neighborhood, running up the hills of Lowellville, picking flowers, and caring for her mother. Pinky was a little spark in nature's eye. If God had a daughter, it would probably be someone just like Pinky. Pinky had the heart of a giant, an angel who fell to earth and never stopped running and hopping like the rabbits who picked the strawberries from Mrs. Orlando's garden. "Pinky, get those little bunnies, they have my prize strawberries." "They love your garden Mrs. Orlando. God made them too."

As a young child, Pinky was her mother's companion, often helping with housework as the men in her family went to war. All of her uncles saw action- in the Pacific, at Pearl and on the shores of Normandy as death, destruction and hopelessness gained a footing halfway around the world. Yet Pinky, young, energetic and by definition an "innocent", was hidden deep inside the protective arms of her village. She was the light in the war-time tunnel of darkness, having been touched by the hand of God himself.

"Dance and twirl again little Pinky. Make it all go away." Yet as she danced and twirled into a young little girl of ten or so, Pinky sensed her father, the most beloved person in her young life, was not feeling well. She danced for her father. "Watch me dance Papa, I can't stop, I love it. Watch me twirl, watch me spin around like a wheel!" Her father, one of the most admired men in town, had advanced bone cancer, living in every cell in his body. It had been that way for a while. He was dying longer than he had lived, and Pinky, somehow and in some way, knew it. But she never said a word.

Pinky oozed joy and pure innocence when she accompanied her father to watch her older brother Billy pitch and play in a baseball game. She wasn't quite sure of the rules or what was a good or bad play, but she knew her father enjoyed watching his son, and that made her happy. Other experts in the crowd, "Men of the Game", thought it amusing, as they undoubtedly knew Pinky and their paisan' Dominic were watching a young man who would be a future hall of fame player. When his tough team mates were not looking, Billy would throw a glance or a wave Pinky's way, blowing her a kiss, but covering it up with his pitchers' glove.

Not one good citizen of Lowellville was surprised a bit when Pinky was the charm of her high school class. She loved her young life and everyone she met. Yet with age comes the cruel, little by little, revelation, that not everyone in the world was like Pinky. Growing up, her father always lectured never to hold a prejudice against a person from another race or background. His personal experience as a young boy made that a family rule. The Italian immigrants had gone through a horrible prejudice when they came to America. He would not let his family do the same to others.

Lowellville High School was having its annual Belle of the Ball dance for Pinky's senior year, and Pinky was looking to dance. After all, who could stop that twirling ball of energy. As Pinky was making her dance card, filling in the blank lines with names of all sorts of dance partners she scouted, a young black student, one of only two in the school, occupied a place on Pinky's list. His name was Brandon. Brandon stood silent on the fourth or fifth step of the cement stairway that led to a class they shared. The young Brandon began to cry. "'What's wrong?" "This is going to be a blast, aren't you coming?" The sad young boy, who was only now learning how the world really worked, quietly replied, "No one will dance with me." Nothing is worse than children being cruel to other children. As those words slowly twisted a knife in young Pinky's back, she found another cause of sorts; She became the defender of the oppressed.

Pinky was never one to anger, until now. As her classmates recall, Pinky, in disbelief, approached many of her friends and asked them to sign Brandon's dance card. Most, if not all, refused. He was, after all, "a Negro" living in an Italian neighborhood. In an act of beautiful defiance, Pinky would now take Brandon as her date to the ball. Either all hell would break loose, or something would change. It was that simple. Pinky entered the school with Brandon on her arm. She danced with him all night. She never missed a song or a beat. Brandon was hard pressed to keep pace with her. When he did, he was in such a joyous mood, now being accepted as one of the students, as opposed to the son of a black farmer in Northeastern, Ohio. The electricity Pinky produced during their dances hotwired the entire room. Before the end of the evening, every girl that attended the dance had Brandon on their dance card. Every student was color blind that evening. It was a young person's night, and it would not be disrupted by puzzling and closely held prejudices controlling the tainted hearts of some Americans outside of that small high school in Lowellville, Ohio. Most of the young, shy white students, stuck like cows glued against the walls of the high school gymnasium that evening, eventually asked, no begged-young Brandon to give up his secrets. He did, happily. He was no longer Brandon, "the Negro". He was now, just "Brandon". Pinky loved that.

One day, Pinky watched as her brother Bill went away. She knew he was going off to another place like her uncles and her neighbors. Pinky cried and danced and ran through the green hills of the town, shouting down to the tracks, "Billy come back, I want to see you throw the ball and run around in a circle." "Don't die Billy, please don't die like Mrs. Virtucci's son. She is all alone now."

Billy, with the clothes on his back, headed for the United States Army induction center. He was going to war. As he took a final look back, he could have sworn he saw his little sister Pinky, dancing on a pin, in her own little world. "Be well Pinky, be well."

Chapter V

GOODBYE KOREA

For all the horrors of war America had endured in the first half of the twentieth century, history made them add one more. During the inhumanly brutal fighting between North and South Korea, the United Nations peacekeeping forces, led by the United States Army, assumed the major role in pushing back the Communist tide fueled by North Korea and China. It was 1950, and MacArthur's park was a flashpoint for stopping the spread of Communism. America's young men were heading to war once again. Uncle Sam was calling, and this time, William George Olive was there to answer.

(Historical Notation, left column, yellow legal pad.) "Comfort Girls, or Western Princesses", were young girls forced into prostitution by the armed forces of Japan, as they pushed their fight into China in World War II. Servicing soldiers at the front lines and in other parts of South Korea, these young Korean women were forced into the unthinkable; Sexual slavery at the hands of the invading Japanese soldiers. This barbaric practice would continue with the arrival of the U.S. Army. The United States government noted that in the context of a world at war, "winning", by any means, was accepted. The sexual exploitation of "the innocents" would again be one of those "means." (End Historical notation).

Young Billy Olive, of Lowellville, Ohio, turned in his baseball uniform and asked for another kind. Billy Olive volunteered for duty in the Korean war theatre. Bill Olive, United States Army private first class, was heading for South Korea, and would be stationed in a village south of Seoul. A gray Navy freighter, with its hollowed out tin hull, provided less than hospitable conditions as it transported America's young men across the oceans of the world, docking forty days later at the Peninsula of Korea. Young Bill was tossed in with a hundred or so recruits and volunteers, bunking square on the bottom metal hull of the vessel. Unending bouts of sea sickness, dysentery, and other communicable infectious diseases rotted away the very bodies of those who sought to serve. Bill was with fever. Bill was unable to walk. Bill lost his sense of time. Bill, would in the end, lose his innocence, once again.

Billy Olive, a star pitching prospect from Lowellville, Ohio, had lost forty pounds during this "voyage of the damned." Billy thought he was resurrected when the boat gave up its young cargo to the shores of South Korea. In the final analysis, private Willaim "Billy" Olive was simply trading one form of hell for another. He was attached to the Military Police Unit somewhere South of Seoul. His assigned duties, among others, included a very unique and peculiar task. Pvt. Billy Olive was ordered by his superiors to transport Korean "Comfort Girls", once a month, to the U.S. Army's military hospital, some forty clicks up the road from his post. There, they would be examined by military doctors to prevent the spread of venereal disease among the troops. Pvt. Olive would take forty of these young women at a time, in two trucks, and deliver them to the field hospital for examination and penicillin therapy, if necessary. Over a time, the girls who accepted their lot in hell, began to take a liking to the young M.P., often teasing him, taking notice of his youth and ignorance of war. Under any other circumstances, Private Olive's actions would be criminal. For the women on the front lines of battle, it was just another day in war that would seek to destroy their homeland, Korea.

The normalcy of this agreement blinded this incoming American soldier. The poetry of that time, before the fall of Korea, reflected a much different world. "Young Korean girl, you are the apple of your father's eye, the pride of your family." "Smelling like spring flowers, wearing yellow petals in your hair, a beauty only you could bring to our way of life." Now here come the Japanese; Brutal, animalistic, vicious. Forced into sexual slavery, they now serviced their enemy. The minds of these young girls were traumatized, as if crushed by a cold sledge hammer. " I don't understand. Why do I have to go?" "I am only thirteen. Mother, please help me!"

Japanese soldiers formed lines, and with permission from the authorities, violated their adolescent bodies in ways the "innocents" could not have imagined. Battered and in shock, they were alive, in theory only. Lost in a daze, diseased by a war, they became the walk-ing dead. A single light bulb hanging from an electrical line plugged into a cracked ceiling, provided just enough light to create shadows of the unspeakable acts committed upon them by the Japanese invaders. After a time, the "innocents" came to believe there was only one way out of this surreal torture land. " 어머니는 그들이하는 일을합니다. 이해가 안 돼요 더럽습니다"나는 내일 자살한다. 나는 살고 싶지 않다. 나는 내일 자살한다..." (Translation: " Eomma, (mother) I do not understand. I feel dirty. I.. kill myself.") The innocents surrendered their will to resist, many choosing to die with a morsel of honor still remaining in their soul. As suicide notes to family members were found in unusual places, like messages in bottles tossed into the sea of war, none of these farewell notes made it to the eyes of their loved ones. Japanese soldiers, who were trained to translate the Korean language, laughed. One monster told another monster, " How can they kill themselves when they are already dead?"

On the heels of the Japanese, the new power, the United States Army, had arrived in Korea. A friendlier version of hell for the Western Princes had arrived. A "nicer" version of forced sex and rape, unfurled in a flag with stars and stripes, was the new order of things. Now here comes Billy Olive. He is your friend. He takes you to the doctor. He is part of this circle of hell, in spite of his boyish looks. "I hate you Americans, you killed my people, I hate you Billy Olive; No more needles, no more stinging penicillin." " I slit your throat while you sleep and watch you bleed, pass out, open the eyes of death, and cut off your head." The collective minds and unbridled hate conjured up from the Western Princesses awaited the new man, the new American, William Olive, of Lowellville, Ohio. Yet somehow, out of the total morass and fog of war, he found solace and peace and love and kindness; And her name was Sun-yee.

Upon arriving at the Korean Peninsula, Private Olive lived in a military barracks. The South Korean police occupied one next to Billy's quarters. That particular barracks was utilized by the military police force of South Korea for the interrogation of local civilians, who were suspected of being spies for the North, and possible traitors to the Korean homeland. Like it or not, at all hours of the day and night, Private Olive, as the walls between the two were made of off-white colored paper and air, would lay awake in bed, and listen to unearthly screams and demonic sounds coming from the barracks next door. Billy Olive was able to see through a crack in the paper wall of his barracks. He witnessed acts of inhumanity, war crimes, and worse. On one occasion, with screams unable to ignore, Billy Olive witnessed sights he would never forget for the rest of his days. He watched as his South Korean allies stripped and lay a female suspect down on the ground, beating her to a pulp, using their bare fists, rock hard steel batons and the iron handles of their sidearms as the tools of her destruction. They smashed and bashed her broken eyeglasses into her face, over and over and over again, until the shards of glass and bits of frame became embedded into her purple swollen face and hanging left eye. She was unrecognizable, as a human being, looking more like ground meat in a supermarket back in Lowellville. On another night, the rip in the paper wall revealed a suspect being battered and sliced with the thin steel edge of a shovel, cut up and pulverized, until he stopped moving, permanently. The shrill of the screams would keep Pvt. Olive awake all that night. He thought them animals. But he was new, and his military training taught him to keep his eyes open, but his mouth shut. Yet young Billy Olive, at nineteen years old, came to believe that man's inhumanity to man in times of war, was indeed real and to the young private, it became unbearable to watch.

His status as an M.P. on the back lines in a civilian town came with privileges of any command of this nature. His outfit was in charge of keeping the peace. The last thing the MacArthur forces needed was an outbreak of civilian violence in towns that were near the front lines of Seoul, the place where life met death. Private Olive was doing well learning the ropes. Soon after he left his barracks next to the torture shack, he looked for his own residential quarters in town. War time in Korea, for civilians, was apocalyptic. Their once secure towns and villages were firebombed by the invading North Koreans and Communist Chinese. They did not have food to eat. They had no shelter from the brutal cold during the winter on the peninsula. They had no weapons to defend themselves. They were "the vulnerables." Pvt. Olive, as an MP, had access to all the food the U.S. troops would eat, including ice cream and candy. He used his PX privileges, and some privileges he didn't have, to set up a home for five Korean families. They would live in a crumbling, mud thatched tructures, with small holes cut out of the floors, allowing the warmth, created by the fires set ablaze underneath these invisible edifices, to blanket their children at night. Billy Olive would search for and find cloth and other comfort material for the women to use to make modest beds for their families. His personal mission was making sure these walking casualties of war lived like humans, eating three meals each day and ice cream at night. Billy Olive cleaned up his portion of the world, all while in a hot war zone.

Private Olive, along with his other "duty", was in charge of making sure the local prostitutes were off the streets by 9:00 p.m. It was martial law in full force. If caught, both the U.S. soldier and Korean prostitute would be arrested. The tentacles of death, birthed on the front lines in Seoul, also made their way into the streets of the town. The violence of the war up North was never far away. It was not long before the young private saw his first casualty of war. An American officer was riding atop a military tank when the army vehicle hit an overhead concrete bridge, the tank flipping over, first decapitating the officer, then crushing his entire body. As the tank rumbled through the underpass, the soldier's lifeless body lay there, next to the muddy rice road. Shades of Lowellville flashed back in the young M.P.'s mind.

Billy Olive carried a .45m.m. side arm, and was an expert marksman with a government issued rifle. Some of the bar fights between soldiers and other local non-combatants tended to evolve into out of control riots. Billy Olive's other duty called upon him to extinguish those fires. Bill was a competitor, and even with stripes on, he wasn't going to avoid a confrontation. Another soldier, well out of control with drink, was about to strike Billy on the head with a sharp object. This intoxicated patron had an Ernie Powell hat on, making him all the more a clear target for a marksman. Bill could have delivered "one" to the soldiers midbrain, but instead, shot him in the knee. A week later that same "broken glass wielding private" was discharged. He thanked Pvt. Olive. For many years thereafter, Billy wondered whether the soldier thanked him for not taking his life, or for sending him stateside courtesy of the gunshot to his knee. But for Private Olive, it was just another day, another duty discharged, in the land of the hopeless.

After being "in country" for a month or so, Bill was no stranger to the long, sharp needle filled with penicillin. But he was also not a fan favorite of the local madams. He was "bad for business" as he enforced the code and arrested anyone at an un-authorized house of prostitution. In fact, when he received his discharge orders, one particular "madam" running such an operation was so happy that she gave Pvt. first class Billy Olive "one on the house", something, she said, had not been done in twenty years. These duties as a Military Policeman had placed him into many unusual circumstances. Regarding prostituion, Billy was put in the middle of delicate matters. If an officer of rank was caught with a prostitute after hours, an officer of a higher rank had to come to that location to "bail him out" of the pinch. Here was young Billy Olive from farm town Ohio, catching a Colonel with his pants down after curfew, and spending the rest of the night looking for a United States Army General to get the Colonel's arse out of trouble. As an M.P., for every act he did to fulfill his duty, he made both friends and enemies. In the war culture, he had to learn that insane people employed tactics rooted in despair. The local Korean women were no exception. "Sleep with an American, then kill him." "Go to the club, find the G.I, use him; You need food, you have a child." "Tell G.I. you will do anything, forget your heart, it's gone anyway." "Love is dead, feelings are dead; They could shoot you in the head and you wouldn't take notice as you walked and bled out in the streets South of Seoul." All these things and more were part of William Olive's new reality. He soon began counting the days until his discharge and return to America.

Yet, as enlightened minds know, fate always has its way, no matter the circumstance. Private Olive recalled it was a Saturday night, when he first met her in a military canteen or bar, where soldiers came in search of female companionship. Billy was no different. He remembers it all as if it were a second ago. The Club South, with its purple garish colored walls, broken ceiling fans and bamboo floors, was a smoke shack that night. As he looked across the bar, he saw her, sitting alone. He was awestruck. She was poured into a white dress with yellow flower petals planted in her razor thin black silk hair. Her skin was flawless, her eyes as black as midnight; Her lips colored with a deep red rose. He could feel her young soft flesh from across the room. The petite young woman's body was perfectly curved, as if painted by Michelangelo himself. He saw her smile and light a cigarette. He stared at her until she, in a brilliant move, ignored him. The young private was not discouraged. He walked over to her. He stared at her from head to toe. She was the most beautiful human being he had ever seen. " I am Sun-yee." His thoughts ran wild, as his mind concluded that he didn't care if she was a Comfort Girl or a local looking for someone to watch over her. He imagined speaking to her, " Come home with me, Sun-yee." "I have a place of solace for you, I can protect you, you will not be hungry, you will not be cold, you will never lack a place to lay your body down for a deep sleep." " Come with me, let me love you, let me protect you, the one named Sun-yee."

A month or two later, the two were inseparable. It was a risky, hot romance, two young people in love in the middle of a war zone. They held each other close, merging as one, in between the sounds of nearby bombing and whistling bullets. They walked down the streets of the village, hand in hand, within a shouting distance of men and women who were being torn apart by shrapnel and the weapons of war. But they also took refuge in quiet places. They disappeared into hidden parks, taking long, intimate walks. They made love under the guns of MacArthur. It was intense, it was real and it was something that should have survived the war. But it didn't.

Soldiers in the United States Army at the time were committed to serve one full year in the battlefield of Korea. It was inevitable that the day they both feared would arrive. Their love could not stop the passage of time. William Olive's discharge papers were blunt. He was given a date, and it was not an invitation. He was ordered Stateside. Now, he had to do the unthinkable, tell his beloved Sun-yee, and he did. Upon deciphering the words of another language, Sun-yee broke down in a torrent of tears. " 나는 당신을 사랑합니다 미국 사람, 당신과 함께 데려가주세요 ... 나는 당신과 결혼합니다. 제발 미국 사람, 제발 빌리, 날 떠나 지마 그들은 나를 죽이고 난 당신을 사랑 해요 영원히 !"

(Translation: " I love you American man, Billy. Take me with you! I marry you." "Please American man, please Billy, don't leave me." "They kill me." " I love you American man. Forever.") Billy Olive was leaving the cratered peninsula and sailing the rough waters home, back to America. It was not a suggestion; It was an order by the most powerful government on the face of the earth.

As the military truck pulled away, Private Bill Olive, with his gear plopped down next to his spot on the motorpool truck, shed his first tear, waving to his beloved Sun-yee, as she began running toward the truck, now begging: "Pappa Son, please, I die, please I need you! Don't go G.I.!" Private Billy Olive, as the truck gained speed, leaned over the back of the military truck and reached out his right hand in a frantic attempt to clutch Sun-yee's outstretched arm. He shouted a pledge, over the noise of the trucks grinding wheels and shouts from his commanders, that like MacArthur, he would be back. Yet they both knew it was a lie. He watched as Sun-yee collapsed, falling to the ground as she could no longer keep pace. Her features became a blur with each turning of the truck's wheels. Her beautiful jet-black silk hair, now cruelly smashed into the muddy, urine stained war roads of South Korea, was only the beginning of her transformation. Billy labored to hold back his tears as his fellow soldiers, in an act of respect, looked the other way. One such soldier clenched his arm, pulling it back, so he didn't do something stupid . His heart was in Korea, but his wife was back in the states. He was now in the middle, torn by the forces that he and the war had created. He was a casualty of that war in the most vicious of ways. While wounds of war are healed by the body, a broken heart lasts forever.

In the end, Private William George Olive was given the grace of not knowing the permanent fate of his love, Sun-yee. After Billy had gone stateside, people like Sun-yee were corraled back into the horror of war-time prostitution. People like Sun-yee serviced other American soldiers, and, after a time, became accustomed to their role. She cried for Billy every night, opening her heart and soul, then closing off all feelings during the next day's rapes during the Western Princes' experience. After a time, the war had gone bad for the U.N. group. The Chinese were slothing up toward the North, committing thousands of troops to the Communst cause. Seoul and villages South of it were overrun by the most brutal of North Korean soldiers. Bill would never know people like Sun-yee were violently raped, then murdered by the Chinese army, and by their partners, the demonic North Korean soldiers. He would never hear her silent screams of madness, as her soul was removed from her body. After the war, women like Sun-yee walked around in a permanent daze, staggering, searching for water and food, like the grazing animals they had become. She was often spotted walking the streets at night, not knowing where she was, but silently singing American songs, and softly speaking to someone who was not there. She would suffer the ultimate humiliation, after the war, of being an outcast among her own people. No South Korean man would touch her. The Western Princesses were all marked with a scarlet letter. That was the "reward" for their service in the rape camps. She was denied medical treatment by the new government, as she was falling through the cracks of what remained of civilization. For Sun-yee, there was more catastrophe to come. She had a child as a result of three nights of unrelentless rapes by many soldiers. The child was born blind, untreated syphilis the cause, and shortly thereafter, buried like filthy waste, dumped with other dead bodies and garbage into a mass grave. One American soldier silently confessed to his sergeant, " I hope like hell there is no God, he would kill us all."

Sometime in 1960, (some seven years after the end of the war,) while Billy Olive was leading his new life in America, a hospital ward in South Korea, operated by the Red Cross, provided a chance of resurrection for people like Sun-yee. She was taken in a truck to the new hospital, having been warehoused for months in a hellish jail dungeon which doubled as a psychiatric ward. One night, close to Christmas Eve, Sun-yee was admitted as a patient at this new hospital. Now a mere eighty pounds, with signs of advanced skin and other diseases, she crawled into the corner of her room, and passed away from this life. On the morning following her death, an old army nurse serving in South Korea, who was familiar with the plight of these "patriotic young girls," called for the helpers to put her body in a cloth bed, roll it up, and prepare it for a funeral pyre. Disease ran rampant after the war. Martial law ordered the cremation of all the dead.

The dead, mostly women and children, were tossed in the back of a truck, much like the Western Princesses taken for medical treatment by Pvt. William Olive. This time, they were to be taken to be burnt to ashes. As a young private walked along side of the back hoe that dug the mass grave, he assisted in the unloading of the diseased dead, and prepared them for the funeral pyre. The private noticed one of the bodies had one of its arms slip out of its burial wrapping. He put on rubber gloves to place the arm back in place. Rigamortis had caused this disruption. In the middle of this duty, as he twisted her rigored arm back onto the pile, he noticed an ink tattoo, the kind many wore to honor their American boyfriends that treated them like humans. After looking at the tattoo with a heart and the inscription of "Billy O." imprinted into its flesh, he dumped the remains into the pit. A furious fire was lit and witnessed miles away. The smell of burning dead flesh sickened many of the soldiers. The price of war spares no one.

In the final analysis, although Billy Olive wanted to reach out and whisk Sun-yee away with him on that fateful day, the realities of life commanded otherwise. Billy Olive now had only one choice, only one thing he could do with the awesome pain that would now, and for the rest of his days, sear his soul; He just had to live with it. There was no other way.

Chapter VI

COMING HOME

First class Pvt. William Olive arrived in port, stateside, sick and underweight from the journey home. Soon a bus and a train would roll him back to Lowellville where his wife awaited him. He was finished with his passion, baseball, as his left arm muscle had atrophied after its injury. His grandfather was gone and his cancer ridden father needed help with the family roofing and gutter business. Bill would go back, if only for a while, to work on the gutters and rooftops at the homes of his neighbors. Yet while he began to attempt to assimilate back into the pace of civilian life in small town America, he became restless, in both body and mind. He never really had a transition from youth to adulthood. He skated over that rite of passage quickly. It was school then war, and now back to his interrupted youth. His classmates who, for one reason or another, were not called upon to serve in Korea, were also in a restless mode. It was 1953, and America was changing. The pace and energy of the post-war country bubbled over into the four corners of the country. There had to be an escape, a place or way of life, for the release of this pent up energy of these young people. Something new, something both dangerous and exciting was in the air, and Billy "O", like the hounds he used while tracking prey in the woods of Pennsylvania, smelled it. Maybe it was his brush with death in Korea, or the changing of gears after a year of war, but there was no denying that young Bill had to do something else with his life; He would be an old man soon enough. Forty years of gutter and patching work, while honorable, was not on his short list. Something had changed.

Youngstown, Ohio, and the Lowellville area, both in the same county, were experiencing a post-war boom. A young man could fall out of bed in the morning and be working at one of Youngstown's five steel mills before noon. The money was good and it was a stable income for raising a family and moving into a home. Bill had tried that, as many of his age had, but the hole in the donut was missing. Now, without sports, there was no adrenaline kick to snap him out of his depression caused by his loss of Sun-yee. Fleeting anxiety, angst and a sore neck from being whipped around the world made him a virtual "jack in the box". Rock n' Roll, rattling up and out in America didn't do it for him either. Elvis was low energy for Billy "O'. What Billy needed was something different, something new. Billy "O" needed to rumble fast and hard, and he needed to do it now.

Chapter VII

MOBTOWN

I t was in their D.N.A.; Youngstown was called little Chicago, after the Al Capone experience. The town once known as the "King of Steel" would later capture headlines as "Mobtown USA" or "Crimetown USA." Eighty-two bombings, sixteen in one year, blew the town sky high, along with buildings, cars, gangsters and their girlfriends, all coming down in the late 1950's and early 1960's. "Bombtown" was booming. The La Cosa Nostra was going strong. The "bug," once a "take it or leave it pastime," was now a red hot street lotto game, paying incredible purses, all on the roll of a dime or the toss of a hat. Anyone could be a winner, or so the public thought. But the real winners of the game were the mobsters themselves. The "bug" provided a flood of cash for the support of the mob's other enterprises, such as prostitution, gambling, extortion, murder and eventually, yes, the drug trade. While Bill enjoyed the thrill of being a numbers runner back in his short youth, he was a bit tired of taking orders, having his fill in Korea. Bill now liked to do things his own way. He was the early alpha male, a born again maverick by definition, and if he wanted the excitement of quick money or a thrill, he would do it on his own terms.

Many of Bill's buddies from his hometown were now low-level members of the local "La Cosa Nostra." Corruption, organized and disorganized crime, short cuts, the easy way, the wise guy way was for many, the only way to go. Youngstown, Ohio, to be clear, was and is home to the hardest working people in America. It was a town built upon the back breaking labor of immigrants who came to the United States in the early part of the twentieth century. Once arriving at Ellis Island, Southern Italian immigrants either stayed in New York City, or migrated to Pittsburgh, Pennsylvania, Youngstown, Ohio, or Cleveland, Ohio, to fulfill the heavy demand for excellent workers in the steel industry. During most of the twentieth century, ten percent of every piece of steel used to build the United States into a super power was manufactured at five major steel plants, all located on the banks of the Mahoning River, in the greater Youngstown, Ohio, area. Yet, one of the deep regrets of many, including the Italian people who came here to fulfill their dreams, was the unwanted migration of these organized crime families from Southern Italy. They were brutal, bold, heartless and notwithstanding popular movies about them, populated by dishonorable men. Billy Olive himself, neither a complete sinner or saint, made it a point to stay away from their influence and corrupt power, all centralized at ground zero in Youngstown, Ohio.

The most disturbing outcome of the migration of these types, who were and are a disgrace to the Italian people, was the infiltration of their damning values over the years. The culture of Youngstown, Ohio, was influenced by the very presence of it. This corruption reached out and "owned" Mayors, Judges, Police Chiefs and Public Officials. The culture of organized crime was embedded into the social fabric of the entire surrounding county. Gambling, Prostitution, Extortion and Murder were the mob's calling card. You could bust your back in the steel mills or related industry, and maintain your character, or work for the Mafia. Those were the only choices.

The most difficult part of "it" was that something like the seemingly harmless as bug" street gambling lottery, became the entrance point, the gateway and a welcoming front door to life long ties with the mob. Most damaging, the "bug" operation involved the use of many, many people, including young teenage kids, who worked as "runners", dispatching them to numerous and varied locations to pick up the betting wagers for the week and bring them back to the mob "bank", or a designated collector. Being a young "bug runner" either alone, or with Uncle Paolo, planted the idea in a young man's mind that minor violations of the law, like being a "runner" for the bug men, was a cool thing. They felt empowered at a young age with the few dimes and quarters tossed their way for a day's work. Connecting with the organization early in life provided many young immigrant kids with an identity, one they wanted to keep, as they matured in life. It was common and accepted that young street kids would become numbers runners during the depression, and would continue to do so well into the 1970's. It was as normal as watching a Baseball game. Young people growing up in the Valley would never know the difference between right and wrong. If uncle Tony or cousin Carmen said it was harmless, how could it be otherwise? It was, in the end, an easy transformation from the harmless life of a bug runner, as a young boy, to a life of crime.

In between the swings and pitches on the Baseball fields of Northeastern Ohio, and while working an honest job with Pops and his father Dominic, Billy was drawn in and given a taste of the water of that world. As a naive' companion of a family friend who helped collect "bug money", to servicing the mob owned vending machines with his uncle, Billy saw more and more of that part of life. In his senior year at Lowellville High School, a lifelong friend recalled that young Bill purchased the bottom part of a duplex, turning it into a hangout for his high school pals, while renting the upstairs bedroom to a divorced mill worker. Billy "O", as his old and new friends began to call him, made sure the party room in the lower level had vending machines which would produce money for his pocket. This once shy, underachiever, was now a "somebody" among his school mates. He liked that. This move by young Olive was either an aggressive preview of a future business tycoon, or the beginnings of a cheap mafia type. No one at that time knew for sure which was the real "tell" for young William Olive's future.

Billy Olive, fresh from his other worldly experience in Korea, was back among his friends who were now established in that culture. They were the only people he knew. Although his grandfather and family raised him to be an honest man, Billy was at high risk of being drawn into "the life." Young Billy was, in retrospect, caught between two worlds.

Yet, violence was the calling card of the mafia. It smeared the great name and reputation of this town of immigrants. Billy, later in life, often commented that "most of the bombings were not related to mafia business, but to personal vendettas." Billy Olive thought the outfit was short on brains, and run by thug enforcers. He steered clear of them. He would work with them, but not for them.

Over the four decades that Billy Olive and the rooftoppers operated, they were outsiders, mavericks, not bound by the rules of violence governing the Mafia. While Bill had his three main crew members for all those years, it was necessary to take, from time to time, a different fourth man into the fold. Billy Olive was good with numbers. Among the hundred or so "temporaries" utilized from 1953 onward, 29 of these part timers would leave his crew and return to the La Cosa Nostra as street enforcers, connected with Pittsburgh or Cleveland and the five crime families in New York City. They would never come back. These 29 goodguys, some "made members" of the Mafia, while fulfilling their oaths of omerta and committing violent acts in the Youngstown and Warren, Ohio area, became themselves victims of their own violent organization. Many of them were shot by rival family "enforcers." Many of them were in charge of turning on the motor vehicles for their bosses, only to be blown to bits with their body parts strewn all over a neighborhood lawn. (Thus, the phrase, "the Youngstown tune-up" came about.) Some were too ambitious, and were marked for death by higher ups. This life they chose, in the "La Cosa Nostra," should have been listed on their death certificates as the "official cause of death."

Bill and his crew were family men of a different order. They would only pull heists at unoccupied commercial buildings. It was all about money, not blood and revenge. Billy "O" would often say, "We take money from the Insurance Companies. Many times, the retail stores would inflate their loss after a heist. The Insurance company would increase its premiums. It was a stock market type thing, nothing personal." Bill entered a life unlike the thugs that ran the streets, many of them textbook sociopaths. They had no feelings of remorse for anything they would do, including murder. They were incapable of acts of kindness, regardless of the portrayals on television and film. They were self-centered, dangerous narcissists. In their world, it was always what was in it for them. They considered the people of Mahoning County expendable, if they interfered with business. These people would not, and did not think twice about pulling the trigger and killing anyone who opposed them. Some of these gangsters who knew Billy Olive thought that maybe "it was something he saw during the Korean War" that made him refuse to participate in violence. It would be a guess, as Billy never spoke very much at all about the horrors he witnessed. But in the end, it could have been a guess that just might have been right.

Chapter VIII

THE FINZIO'S CAPER

O ne could imagine the energized rattle and quickly hushed
conversations of five or so young men from the neighborhood, pumped full of testosterone, looking to fit in, wanting to make a fast buck, impressing a girl- all while drinking at Billy's
street level bar. They would talk about pulling off heists, planning the
various stages of the job after targeting the store, warehouse, bar or
retail shop. It would become as regular as the sun coming up each
morning. "That place on S. Main St., "Finzio's", with the black and
red awnings, you know, the one with the new cars parked out front
on Saturday night, it's perfect and always crowded on weekends."
"Yeah, weekends, they have the big take, cash on a barrel, payroll
time." "I know the kid who works there, they keep the cash under
the third drawer, in the back. Pull out the drawer and it's taped under
the bottom." "Now Benny, you watch for anybody coming around the
corner. I can get Joey to pick the locks, it's easy. Sometimes they never
even lock the doors!" "The sister of that girl you were with, Sophia or
something..she works there; Am I right?" "They have five hundred

bucks in that drawer every Saturday night!" "That's a hundred or so a piece." "No, a little less. The other piece goes to the kid working the tables inside, and the owners son. He hates working there too." No one was ever sure when all the big talk turned into the fast walk. But somewhere back in time, the local kids from the neighborhood became the very best "Heist Crew" West of New York City, and Billy "O" became the leader of that band.

Billy and his young crew broke into this home style eatery as they had planned weeks ago. As they rumbled through the back door, the young crew knocked over a kettle containing homemade pasta sauce and meatballs. That was more of a crime then breaking into the premises! The thick, homemade pasta sauce spilled all over the marble tiled floor. They were heart broken. "Look over in the corner, Billy". Billy saw a huge wheel of old-world Italian cheese, wrapped around what looked like a truck tire. Maybe it was a sign. Billy rolled it out and took it home. He spent hours grating the cheese, meticulously peeling it off of the wheel. "Finzio's ah.! That was a real wheel of cheese." In the end, the grated cheese filled fifty quarts of glass jars. The crew sold them at half price to Italian people on the block. It was biblical! You had to have cheese on your Sunday pasta. But the crew had to answer to the man upstairs for wasting that pure, tomato based pasta sauce. In Italia, what they did was and still is considered a horrible crime, punishable by death. After confessing this to a local priest, they each received ten "Hail Mary's" and one "Our Father" as penance for that mortal sin. Billy and the boys, out of respect for the owner, cleaned up their mess and swept the floor before they parted. They were raised with respect. There would be more jobs to follow, but nothing as close to their hearts as this one.

The boyz in that hood had one caper, one heist, one "hit" under their belt. It was their first taste of easy money. It was 1954 and it was time to rumble.

Chapter XIX

UNCLE MILTIE

T elevision was the biggest hit at the 1939 New York's World's Fair. Many thought it would be used for education and as a replacement for the classroom. But with the end of the wars, the American people were ready for a little fun, laughter and entertainment. This wish would be fulfilled in the form of a little box which flickered images of comedy routines featuring Lucille Ball, Sid Caesar and the famous stars of the day. It was all the rage. Good, affordable televisions were hard to come by in the early days, and for many American families, were beyond their budget. Yet, in the those early days of television, whether watching from a neighbor's home, whose father was a doctor or lawyer with money to buy "the tube', or pressing your nose against a store front window, pushing and inching toward the smudged glass pane for a better view, all of America agreed on one thing; They loved this new "thing" called television, and Zenith made the best. Billy Olive agreed with that sentiment too.

Chicago businessmen Ralph Mathews and Karl Hassel had no way of knowing that their small radio manufacturing and research company would produce, by the early 1950's, the most sought after product in America; The Zenith television set. The young crew of Olive's Company, fresh off the Finzio's caper, decided it was time to get into the television business, but in a new way. Billy's military training as an M.P. taught him that any unit needed at minimum, four soldiers, one designated as an advance scout, one as a lookout, one with technical skills to get the job done, and one for extraction strategies. Every hardware and retail store had zenith televisions for sale in Mobtown USA, Youngstown Ohio. The prices that were out of reach for the average family were about to be discounted. Joe Pinter was an expert at lock picking. They never taught that skill in shop class at Lowellville high school, but he learned his trade as he served an apprenticeship with a crew from one of the Youngstown crime families. Billy "O" himself was the ideal advance man, a recon or patrol officer, having had the responsibility of foreseeing potential harm to army regulars and civilians back in a town South of Seoul, Korea. Benny was a natural exit strategist. He had four ways to Sunday to rumble out of a retail store or such other place if need be. Rocky was the designated scout and was multi-tasked into an inventory control man.

A day or so before a Zenith "discount sale" was set for launch, the crew, including Billy "O" as the advance man, went to the television store's location, police scanner in tow, and monitored the patterns of the police cars and patrolman on the beat in the general area.

Police scanners, for some odd reason, were readily available to the public for most of the 1960's and 1970's. Many elderly people back in that day, including, now that I think of it, my grandfather, used to enjoy listening to their police scanners at night. Ordinary citizens could keep track of the movements of the police officers as they chased runners of red lights down the street, or did a back and forth about a possible garage break-in involving a lawn mower. It was exciting to them. But there was more. It provided a soothing atmosphere, often like a lullaby, putting them to sleep. Billy "O", also a big fan of police scanners, had one of his own. But, as times would reveal, he had a much, much different use for these amazing devices.

"Unit 311, where is code "8" today." "No, where is lunch today, sorry." "Chief what are priority patrol patterns tonight." "My wife has to get her hair done later today, so I need to know Charlie." After a time, Billy knew their first names and which commercial properties they would patrol that evening. When Bill signaled for the rest of the crew to launch their nighttime raid, a respectable hole was quietly made into the back of a large store carrying row after row of Zenith televisions. They would bring a blockbuster, a steel wrecking ball of sorts, for their rather unimaginative entry strategy. Bamb! The cement would buckle and at least one or two neighbors, a few blocks away, would think they heard something strange, a thump of sorts, that woke them from their sleep. But it all grew quite after that, as those nearby neighbors went back to neverland.

Locks in those days were simple enough to pick, but borrowing a semi-tractor trailer to carry away the many television sets at the site, was quite another. When the signal was given, the hole was breached and carts with rollers were loaded with television after television, then pulled up by a conveyor and loaded onto a tractor trailer container waiting in the hushed back of the store. It was a smooth operation. It was done with razor-like precision. It was as efficient as the factory line that put the parts of the zenith creation together. Most people sleep at night, and stores are closed. Billy "O's" crew, however, worked the night shift, at least five times a month.

Billy Olive, while the zenith parade continued up the lift, was filling his duffle bag with money from the store's safe. The guts of it were laying on the floor. He put his hands in and lifted the rubber band holding the dirty paper with dead presidents on it. The noise outside suddenly stopped. A television on display, on the lower level, could be now heard in all its clarity. The theme of the television show "Dragnet"was blasting across the way, with the voice over of crime fighter Jack Webb in the background. It may have been the only time Billy laughed that night, noting the irony of it all, while being scared shitless, at the same time, by that damned thumping "Dragnet theme."

After a good twenty-two minutes, over one hundred televisions were rolled off the showroom floors and into the dark semi-tractor trailer truck. The "marketing consultant", or "fence" for the team had a location for the delivery of the Zenith televisions. They would be sold at half price, smoking hot. The "fence" or middleman would then sell them to various members of the consuming public, with an adjusted retail price that was still far below what a new set would cost during daytime store hours. When the load was too much for the middle man, the rest of the sets were sold to various vendors on the streets at one third the prices of a new set. Billy's crew had the perfect mark up for these sets. Their cost of acquisition was only a few hundred bucks in bribe money for the night guard and the dispatcher who told them where they could borrow a truck for the night. The cost of the sets taken was zero. They were paid fifty percent, pure profit, by the middleman retailer, and 33 and one/third profit by the layoff man. This business model netted the crew a ton of money. To ensure the continuing survival of this operation, Billy Olive had one rule. His crew would always, no matter "the take", split the profits evenly, without fail. There would never be an argument over the division of profits within his new partnership. At the end of the night, after the truck was returned a state or two away, the crew divided the pot. They each made $5,000 dollars. ($50,000 in today's money.) Thanks to Billy and his crew, hundreds of families now had televisions at half price plus, as they enjoyed the season opener of Uncle Miltie with the scurrilous Milton Berle. One barber in a Youngstown suburb, bought so many fenced televisions, that he opened his own retail appliance shop. "It sure beats cutting hair." The "closed" sign was now permanently affixed to his barber shop window. He now had a better way to make money.

Chapter X

THE OLIVE ELECTRIC COMPANY

My mother always got a kick when our friend, Henry, that big red headed kid on the block, listened and watched for the garbage truck to pass through our neighborhood. Something about its odd and shifty design, and the crew that managed it was, to this young kid, quite astonishing. He would always tell my mother, "Mrs. D., when I grow up, I want to be a garbage man." The neighbors would chuckle, as Henry looked for that little monster, like clockwork, on every "garbage" pick up day. (Little did we know in 1965 that a job with a major trash hauler would pay top wages by the time young Henry was in the job market.).

Henry's public utility truck of choice was an Ohio Power Company truck. It rumbled down our pot-holed street, with its mechanical arms waving wildly into the air, like a wounded sea monster, blown apart by cross winds. It would arrive usually on the day after a huge storm, raising its power ladders that would stretch these mechanical arms to the sky, untangling tree branches leaning into electrical wires and telephone poles. Utility men with shiny tools hanging from their brown leather belts were hoisted up into the air, clutching onto a basket of some sort as they hid beneath their off-white helmets. "O.K. Jimmy, just a little higher, ho! Too high, now back it down, a little to the left, O.K. good, give me the hook." With tools in hand, they untangled the sparking twisted electrical wires connected from the pole to homes and businesses. This was an event that all the neighborhood would watch. Although commonplace, it was exciting for the kids.

Northeast Ohio had more than its share of tall trees and large, long branches that would twist in the wind and break off in gale force events. These utility trucks logged many miles. Large public enterprises, like utilities, and specifically the power companies, were closely monitored by the state for their quality of service to the public. When their carefully maintained maintenance sheets indicated their mobile, crane-hydraulic trucks were at a stage of being no longer useful or unsafe, the company was ordered to do what any government would do with an overused, unsafe vehicle; They ordered it sold at public auction, so some other citizen had a chance to be injured by its out of control mechanical spider arms, possibly capturing and squeezing one of the neighborhood kids on some summer evening.

Billy "O" always had a creative mind. Putting it to use for the benefit of society, was a much more complex issue. The state advertised that these used utility trucks, which could not be mistaken for a Camaro or Lincoln continental, would be sold, at least one of them, at a sheriff's sale during the upcoming month. "Benny, check with the Sheriff and see what the bid price is, the starting bid for one of those trucks, the one's the power company's are selling." "Those trucks are too slow and bulky Bill, we rumble in one of those, the cops can catch us on horseback!" "We are going to put a bid in, and get a hold of Jilly, the one who knows the painter, tell him to meet me at the riverboat restaurant tonight, and use the pay phone!" "Always use the pay phone!" "You get it, I am calling you on a pay phone, you know why?" "Did they shut your phone off Bill?" "Come on Bill, you lost that much money at the track?" Benny wasn't the smartest of the bunch.

Billy Olive had an idea. But first he had to get past his wife, Olive Olive. "Where are you going Bill?" "Olive, don't wait up for me. I have to go, to get some money." "But the banks are closed!" "Just don't wait up, Olive, the bank I am going to has unusual hours." Billy "O" went to reliable people and places and put together the money for the auction, bull headed and with the single purpose of getting that truck; And he did just that, paying cash as high bidder, and in an unceremonious way, driving the son of a bitch right off the auction block. When he contacted his crew to present them with their latest style of travel, they nominated him for time in the local asylum, until Billy had a chance to give one of his short, brief but irrebuttable arguments.

The crew met at an undisclosed location in the backwoods of Lowellville. One of the crew was an artist of sorts. As soon as the purchased utility truck pulled up alongside his paint wagon, he began slapping and sloping white and green paint, without the spill or smudge of a drop, as blurry images began to emerge from his master work in progress. This particular used Electric Company vehicle was green on the top, and parts of its sides, mixed with white and grey, and a trend of red, coated down on the mechanical spider arms that waved wildly on command. The vehicle was indeed used, its paint peeled and stripped after a decade of service in the harsh and blustering Ohio winters and its humidity-soaked summers. If one were to repaint this beast, give it a set of respectable tires and otherwise give it a makeover, it would look "brand spanking new", and that was the point. As the slapper began his Michelangelo imitation, retracing the name of the power truck company exactly as it appeared in the catalogue for vehicles of this type, one could possibly say it was good to go, and could be back in service in a jiffy. Billy "O" and his crew had no intention of getting into the market of "flipping old utility trucks" and reselling them to some other power company. They had, let us say, a much more creative and profitable use for it.

In Youngstown, Ohio, back in the day, you could, as they would say about New York City, get anything you wanted or needed. If you knew which person to reach out to, and Billy did, you could order brand new or very fashionable rehabbed working uniforms for your purchase, ready with a week's notice. Police uniforms, Fire Chief's outfits, garbage men's fashions of the day, or even, yes, power company khaki pants and shirts, with the correct color combination and requested brand name stitched into the shirt of the clothing. The black market had it all, and Youngstown was tied in, all the way, with the black market. It came in handy.

Sometime during the 1960's and 1970's, banks and retail stores began to install electrical "contact" wires to their safes and locks, connecting them to power lines that ran out and up to nearby telephone polls, giving their system the ability to trigger an alarm as loud as a tornado warning siren, to the community and police, when their safes were breached or tampered with. Many people in the industry knew that. Billy did too. A strategy was required to disconnect the alarm system wires from these telephone polls. Those power company servicemen's suits were now ready. The "new" truck was painstakingly examined to make sure that all of its turn signals, lights and blinkers were in perfect order. Billy "O" made sure that the muffler was checked, leaving no probable reason for the law to pull the truck over for a traffic inquiry. Orange cones, those little knee biting monsters, would decorate the new utility truck as it parked in front of the desired location. Billy would need a few of them too.

After discussing the details of the surveillance, the repainted, fixed up, brand spanking new power truck, now registered to some other company in Timbuktu, was put into use. The power company crews, with their repaired and re-stitched uniforms, were ready for a hard day's work. A tree, during an otherwise quiet weather night, had mysteriously fallen on the telephone wires near the local commercial bank in town. (It had 'chop' marks near its roots.) The president of the bank was worried that the potential hazard would dissuade his customers making deposits that day. He was also, to a much smaller degree, concerned about their safety. With Billy's connections to an inside operator, (it's amazing what a hundred bucks did back in the day), his truck was called to "repair" possible wire damage and debris from the tree leaning against the power line. Within minutes of the call to the new power repair crew and truck, Bill's highly trained and skilled wire man was perched in the hydraulic nest that hoisted the wacky and wild arms up to the sky, stopping at the point where the wires, tree and utility pole all gathered. Many of the mothers and children had been attracted to the on goings of the day. They appreciated it very much when one of Bill's safety crew members, putting the orange cones around the truck and directing traffic on the two way road, kindly reminded the mothers, " ladies, please make sure your children stay back, we don't want them getting hit with flying sparks from this wire." The women loved the attention. One of Billy's crewmen, who looked like a young Paul Neuman, didn't hurt these polite efforts.

Benny, one of Billy's favorite boyhood pals, was like a maestro when it came to electrical wires. To him, it was an easy task. For a bit of drama and a reality show type feel, Benny feigned that he was having trouble peeling through the wires, trying to find the correct one to fix the damage caused by the "fallen" tree. The people watching from their front yards, with their kids, didn't care if there was an electrical problem at all, they just liked the excitement. One little girl, Shirley, was selling lemonade to the people standing around and watching in the summer heat. It seemed every little girl back in the day was named Shirley, by parents who suffered during the depression.

Soon enough, another member of the crew came out, declaring to all that the problem had been fixed. The wirey, lengthy spider's arms were brought back down from the sky, and the orange cones removed from the area. As the bank manager signed the receipt for the work done, he profusely thanked Billy "O" for saving the day. It was, after all, a Friday, and that was payday in America, for everyone.

The men, in their brand new power company suits climbed into their official brand-new truck and, with the silent flash of a yellow light, slowly pulled out of the space they occupied. The events of the remainder of the day went on as usual.

The newspaper in that town carried two editions. One edition contained the news of the night before, the "extra" edition, which came out in the early evening, had any important updates the metro area would want to read. One of the mother's that watched the good-looking member of Billy "O's" repair crew, saw her picture in the evening edition, as the "event" was big news earlier in the day. She cut it out and saved it for her friends to read. However, this same local celebrity felt faint when she read the column on the right side of the front page in the next morning delivery. The headlines, "Robbers fool cops, disconnecting bank safe alarm wires from telephone pole", panicked the neighborhood. She had never been that close to real life bank robbers, and she would make it a point to tell of her "brush with criminals" for many years to come.

The amount of cash stolen from that commercial bank, with the modern burglar alarm wired system, was apparently taken later at night, as the safe was removed from the property and whisked away to parts unknown. The amount taken from the bank in question was never revealed by the newspaper, for many reasons, but it was safe to say that only the police, bank officials and Billy "O" could confirm the amount "borrowed without permission" in that caper, and all three of these men, for various reasons, were absolutely silent about the matter. In fact, the only other person that was paid money that day, other than Billy "O" and his power company crew, was the little girl selling lemonade to the bystanders. As for the power company's rehabbed truck and uniforms, Billy "O" had another signature idea. He reversed his earlier decision and sold the truck, with all of its wiley monstrosities and new paint job, to another crew. That weekend, the boyz in that hood headed for their favorite place, Atlantic City. Billy "O" "donated" his entire take of $30,000.00 dollars, in mid-1960's money, to one of the major casinos on the boardwalk. Yet for Billy Olive, a degenerate gambler by his own admission, it was not a wasted trip. "The food was great, and the boardwalk was full of dames from New York City." For now, the crew officially retired from the electrical power company business. Yet Henry, on any given day, still looked for those power utility trucks. Fortune would later smile upon the young red-headed kid from the Southside of Youngstown. He finally realized his lifelong dream. He became a garbage man.

Chapter XI

There's A Semi In Your Drive

Women's fashions were always moved from factories to retail outlets by trucks, on a consistent and regular basis. Bill and his crew would have containers of fashions sold within a day or two, after high-jacking those delivery trucks, and transferring its cargo to various fencing operations. It was that simple. The proper people were given a piece of the action, like the police chief and the warehouse truck dispatcher. What could go wrong?

The tractor trailer rigs, with all their big wheels and shiny tin walls, always ruled the road. The size of the inside of a truck and its attached container, where the goods or products were stored, was much, much larger than anyone would imagine from just looking at the outside of the semi-truck. This was part of the business strategy of the manufacturers. The more dresses they made, or other women's apparel, the more money they would make. Yet it all depended on the speed they could get to market, and the capabilities of their delivery trucks. It was a "truism" that size really did matter.

On the day of the near disaster, all was going according to plan in a major truck heist of some of the most popular women's dresses of the day made by, shall we say, an unknown famous designer from New York City. They were in demand, full tilt. The crew knew hours ahead of time, from their inside source, when the trucks containing the fashions of the day would be leaving the warehouse, what route it would be taking, what truck stops it would use for fuel and rest, and all the relevant details needed for the operation. At the exit on highway 9, the driver of the targeted truck took a break, walking slowly toward the Big Boy restaurant attached to the highway rest area. Locking the doors of the truck was just a minor inconvenience, as the crew picked the lock and hot wired the vehicle before the diver could sit down to order his lunch. Everything had gone perfect that day, except for one thing. The location where the hijacked truck was to be driven and its contents unloaded was now "unavailable", due to the presence of Federal law enforcement vehicles in the area. Billy smelled a rat. Yet, the one time major league baseball prospect, as he was while pitching with the bases loaded, was unflappable. He never flinched, or broke a bead of sweat. Instead Billy "O", in his infinite wisdom, decided he would park and unload the massive tractor trailer truck at his own home, in Lowellville, Ohio, by backing it into his driveway and transferring its contents into his home. "Billy, are you crazy, batz?" "No way that truck sits there without the neighbors calling the cops."

In case you have never been to Lowellville, it is incumbent upon me to tell you that there is simply no way to park, hide or otherwise store a huge, hundred ton tractor trailer truck, fourteen tires and massive container included, height and weight now cracking the blacktop of neighborhood streets, in a driveway in Lowellville, Ohio. It would have been easier to part the Red Sea. First, the houses stood, as it was part of their charm, closer together than two lovers on their honeymoon. Second, the streets of the neighborhood and driveways were not made to hold thousands of tons of steel, without buckling and causing the load and truck to shift, possibly rolling it over and smashing into one of the houses on the many street corners. Third, despite the friendliness of the neighbors, and their love for Billy's family, there was always the risk of one nosey visitor or someone with an ax to grind, calling the local police. (Under normal circumstances, that would not be a problem, as the chief was in for an equal piece of the action.) However, at this time, as they received late but trustworthy word from their toll booth lookouts, the Federal people were patrolling an area that was very, very close to the residence of William George Olive.

Yet Billy's choice of the temporary warehouse location, which involved parking this beast in his driveway, was irreversible. He was now more concerned about how fast he would be able to unload the four hundred or so women's dresses stacked in the semi, smash them into the four corners of his humble residence, and remove them at a later time so they could be sold on the black market for a very healthy profit. He was after all, a businessman, not a socialist.

His crew, in one of the few times they second guessed his judgment, became "masters of the obvious", pointing out to Billy that his truck was sticking out like a sore thumb in this charming little residential area, and that this was no place to unload its precious cargo. Bill, looking at them with a firm smile, quipped "Fellas, let's get started. Unload these dresses, now! Get them into the house, and park the damned truck right here. No one is going to cause me trouble!"

Billy "O" had a respectable home, not too big, not too small. He had a kitchen with a washer and dryer for Mrs. Olive Olive, a fair sized, but not too big dining room decorated with a large oak table, and three bedrooms with queen size beds and matching dresser drawers. In a normal universe, where principles of mathematics and square footage would apply, Billy "O" would have been laughed out of physics class for his "dress stuffing" suggestion. But for two hours, his crew stuffed crammed every single dress in the semi-container, without exception, into the interior of his home. From the top of the ceiling to the bottom of the floor, the merchandise was gently placed and squeezed together like a large multi-colored sandwich. From the kitchen and into the dining room, turning left into the living room, and upstairs toward the bedrooms- and all nooks and crannies in between, his humble home was transformed into a warehouse. Every square foot of the home was utilized. The house had dresses now, hundreds of them, lining its interior. It was a hoarder's dream gone wild. You would need a map to find a pathway through the house. There was barely room for air. The crew had to stay at separate hotels overnight, and Billy's wife had to be diverted from coming home from shopping to her sister's house for an overnight stay. Amazingly, to everyone but Bill, not a tear in a seam, nor a missing sequin or a smudge of grease would be found on these fashions of the day. They were in the same pristine condition as they were when manufactured. They were indeed immaculate, and ready for resale.

As the crew vacated the premises, leaving the super truck and four hundred ladies dresses jammed into every square inch of his home, the Feds were on the prowl. They had been given some good information, from an inside source of their own. They knew who they were looking for, and where he might be living, and were only seconds behind closing in on Billy Olive. It didn't help matters that an artist's sketch of his face, accompanied by his first name, was now hanging on the wall of post offices in a five state area. I often look back and chuckle at the possibility of a fuller brush man or Jehovah witness knocking at the door that afternoon, looking into the front window to see if anyone was home. That "look" on their face would have been priceless.

The next morning, with the balls of an elephant, Billy brought his crew back to his house and had them remove every dress and sweater, occupying every square inch of his home, placing the garments into various cars and smaller trucks that pulled up, in broad daylight, in front of his home. This went on all day Monday. Finally, sometime early Tuesday morning, the last of the dresses were pulled through Billy's back door, (an act very similar to removing a cork out of a champagne bottle,) and driven to its new home, somewhere on the east coast. The boys had performed a minor miracle. On Wednesday, while Bill was getting ready to leave for work at his family's gutter and roof repair business, he was stopped as he walked out the back door. His driveway was not blocked with a semi-tractor trailer any longer, but with three identical Chevy Impalas, brown in color, with red stenciled plates. Six young fleshy-faced lads, fresh off the farm in Quantico, Virginia, all dressed in black suits, began yanking out badges from inside their hidden suit pockets. "Mr. Olive, we have a few questions we would like to ask you." Billy "O", stepping over a chunk of cement uprooted from his driveway, headed for his vehicle parked in front of his house. "Gentlemen, I would like to talk to you, but I have to be at work. Have a good day." Billy "O" was made of brass, and that included everything.

Chapter XII

"Do The Math"

B illy's crew took the truck and their "travelling car", (They used 20 or so cars every few years, all beaters, dumping them after a job,) and headed back to Struthers, Ohio, after another successful outing. The lead tractor trailer used Pennsylvania plates during the stretch through Pa. You had to. If the Pennsylvania State Troopers saw out of state plates, you would be pulled over, just because. "When we hit Ohio, you could switch to Ohio plates or keep the commonwealth plates on." Ohio didn't care either way. Just don't have a blinker or headlight out. And Billy was O.C.D. (obsessive) when it came to this.

The backup car took a different route, no toll booths, on its way back to Ohio. It had to make sure it was about a half hour behind the lead truck. Even though it was a beater, Billy "O" made sure its engine was in good shape, no breakdowns on the freeway in the middle of the night, no flickering headlights or burned out brake lights. Everything had to be perfect; And it was. They made it to a friend's house in Struthers, Ohio, and stored the goods overnight. It would be sold to a middle man in the morning, probably from New York, where he would resale it to people he knew. Some of the merchandise would be kept by Bill himself, and sold on the local streets at a third of the cost. Bill's cost was the gas money, the hotel and meals. It was a successful business model.

The crew did this at least two to three times a week, each year, for, let's say, forty straight years. "Every weekend, without exception, we had a planned heist." It was like working a regular job, except they had no pension or health insurance. Yet, their successful streak was not only incredible, but also verifiable. It could be documented. Think about it for a minute. When the crew did two jobs in a week, that's approximately one hundred heists a year. They did this for approximately forty years; and that is being very, very conservative. My high school teacher would often say, "Just do the math." Well, on this one, 100 jobs a year, multiplied by forty years is approximately 4,000 heists. The average "take" on a heist was over $10,000.00. A certified statistician calculated the odds of performing a task successfully, four thousand times in a row. The odds of that kind of perfection are 4000:1. Imagine those kinds of odds in a horse race. Billy would.

Chapter XIII

Billy "O" And The Blackhearts

B illy "O" was also an equal opportunity employer. On one occasion, he decided to work with an "all girl band." (Joan Jett would have been his biggest supporter.) A group of experienced shoppers, who all happened to be women, decided they would form a gang of their own. Who they were and where this monumental decision was made is not important, but their penchant for shopping at a very, very, very well-known shopping retail outlet, made them experts on what was where, what shelf it was on, whether a ladder was required to reach the item and what new products were coming into the loading docks. That particular outlet, known for its lack of, shall we say, staff, to assist customers, could have done the shopping public a solid by hiring these gals as floor reps, or customer service reps or as a "why can't I find someone who knows where to find this and that...no one is ever here...!" reps. Yet this outfit, these shoppers, were not interested in working for the chain, nor were they interested in doing actual "transactional shopping" at the chain. (Where one pays for the merchandise they take from the store.). These gals were not interested in any of that kind of work. In fact, they became the architects, pioneers of a sort, of the retail chain's "Home Delivery" program.

Sure, any two bit thief could hustle out everyday items, and they did, such as razor blades, soap, shampoo, toothpaste, candy, women's tops, shoes, garden seeds, and a ton of other commodities, slipping them inside places only ladies know about, walking out as if they were valued customers, greeting the greeters and ignoring the greeters on the way out; But they had a different plan. They would sell these items on the streets of their neighborhoods. People needed everyday sundries or items that would save them a few cents on the dollar. The girl gang had customers, regular ones. It was a business model that was more reliable than Amway. The neighborhood clients simply would make their lists, give them to their shoppers, and the ladies of the day would visit the huge store, and return, personally delivering the ordered items to their front door, at half price.

There would come a time when Billy and his crew discovered this girl band and became one of their "distributors" in certain parts of the state. These women were excellent business partners. They were steady and delivered their cargo on time, and as requested. Yet, it was only later that Billy "O" discovered that this female band had another expertise, another way of moving merchandise off the floor and into the hands of the eager public. The "Blackhearts" had a special set of skills with regards to the "lay-away" program used by this retail giant. This "go to" platform was always available to those not willing to pay the usury interest payments charged by credit card companies. The lay-away program permitted a shopper to select an item, box it, and put it behind the shelf, as you made a payment or two and picked it up another day.

The curly que crew would plan shopping days at various locations of these stores. They were careful not to form a pattern detectable by a mall cop. The girls would simply haunt the isles of the big box stores, almost like daytime ghosts, and look for higher end items that they wanted to sell to fences, after they pilfered them out of the stores. The all female crew would put jewelry, watches, higher end fashion, and small high end items in a box that was "marked" as a "$29.99 sweeper". The box was long. The box was wide. But this box, instead of containing the cheap "made in China" carpet sweeper described on the front, was filled with inventory such as jewelry, men's watches, rings, ready to wear accessories, several higher end sweaters, over the counter medication in demand, you know, things that would cost a thousand bucks, all wrapped up and put in a $29.99 layaway box- and put to bed on some dusty shelf in the store's lay-away section. A small storage fee, and a due date was put on the item, and they were ready to go.

The day would come when the crew went "in-store" to pick up the cheap ass carpet sweeper, made in China, that would break in a week or two, that was waiting for them on the "lay-away" shelf. The Blackhearts, now with the help of Billy's crew and their connections to major fencing operations, were set to make a boatload of money. Here comes Billy "O" and the Blackhearts, doing ten stores at a time, in a two state area. Pretty soon those nifty lay-away items were bringing in thousands a week, tens of thousands a month, and the fence, the middle man dealing in these items, sold them from Ohio to the East Coast. Billy, true to his creed, paid everyone equally, including the girls. He was an equal opportunity employer and a champion of women's rights in the workplace, all before it became a political talking point.

Chapter XIV

"WHO KNEW?"

O
ne policeman in our family used to say, "It's never boring, you never know what is going to happen; It's something new each day." If anything, this applied a hundred times over to Billy and the boys. You never knew where the next opportunity would come from.

Early on, one particular bar, where a younger Billy "O" was collecting coins from vending machines, had a condom machine inside the lady's room. The machine was rigged. It took the money ladies put in but never produced anything when you turned the handle. It ate the coins every time, by design. Back in the day, although women were beginning to practice safe sex, who would they complain to when the machine didn't work? Most, if not all of the ladies were too embarrassed to ask the male bartender to reimburse them for the money they lost on "that condom machine." Imagine, deep in their mind, the fear of the potential for the bartender, a cat named Skatz, to yell back at Sammy in the kitchen or at the owner having lunch with a bunch of men, "Hey Charlie, the lady here had her coins eaten by the condom machine inside the women's restroom. Third time this week. I thought we fixed that?" Picture the bartender asking the local patron leaning on the bar, in a chair next to where the lady was sitting, "Hey Joey, do you have any condoms you could lend this lady?" "How big? I don't know. Hey doll, who are they for, I mean, do you need large, medium or small?" By this time, she is denying she said anything at all, and after ten minutes of a condom hunt, she would, herself, be taking a tire iron to the machine and removing it from the ladies restroom. "Sorry lady, can't help ya, you're just going to have to take a chance, I guess." Katz would never, ever see that woman again. So much for repeat business!

One Monday, arriving with all of its dreariness, caught the crew in an awkward situation. It was a post office heist. They had good information. They entered and compromised the safe, while the four of them emptied its contents into four separate duffle bags. The safe was a major hit. It contained cash, coins, some jewelry, although they could not figure out why, but most of all, it had stamps, and plenty of them. Now greed is never a good thing and Billy knew it. Yet, in his lust for more, he broke his own rule. Bill knew there were more stamps and cash that could fit in a fifth duffle bag, the four being full. He made the mistake of coming back with another duffle bag, for more stamps and cash. As he approached the opened safe, a light was spotted shining from outside of the exchange during this pre-sunrise operation. The dreaded night patrolman, finishing his shift, had stumbled upon them. The crew had to rumble, leaving behind four bags worth of cash and stamps estimated at $30,000.00. "That was the one that got away." There would be more.

Nebraska is a long, long drive from the farms of Northeastern, Ohio. There is a lot of real estate between these two worlds. Bill would only take his crew on that thousand-mile deal when a reliable source, and he had one, tipped him off that a safe containing payroll for half of the west coast at that time was just sitting there in some cornfield, outside of Lincoln. The local lieutenant of the Pittsburgh mob, now deceased Mafia boss Joey Naples, provided that information. Joey was the man in Youngstown for a very long time. His brothers, prior to their untimely and unnatural deaths, trained Joey in the "ways". Mr. Naples, as he was called by most of the Youngstown area residents, had connections all over the United States. The Pittsburgh outfit and its New York "Supervisors" had that kind of reach.

The crew saddled up and drove across the grand contours of our homeland. Now the place of the heist in Nebraska, for certain, was sparse in population. There would not be any "rubber necks" causing them a headache during this effort. All of the people on the crew, both inside the payroll operation, and outside lookouts and support staff, were in place well in advance of their arrival. The caper was coming down on Billy's signal. The informant recruited by Joey Naples, all the way back in Youngstown, Ohio, was right on the money. The safe, containing hundreds of thousand dollars, if not much more, sprouted out of the farmland of Nebraska like a tall stalk of golden corn. The best safe crackers in the business were on Billy's crew. Nothing was left to chance. In the course of our lives, when we have the utmost confidence in the success of something, a freaky incident or unforeseen factor appears, like a thief in the night, and tosses a monkey wrench into the wheels of fortune. In Nebraska, these rules of the universe, the room for random chance and bad luck, were operating in full force that night. Although the information provided was right on spot, no one could predict the presence, minutes before the "green light", of an unknown, local visitor.

A milkman from a local dairy farm, delivered his product at the crack of dawn each Nebraska morning, to all of his destinations, without fail. On the day of the Olive invasion, the milkman had a busy schedule, picking up the route of a co-worker who was on vacation. He decided he needed a very early start, as in 3:00 a.m. "early", instead of 5:00 a.m., to get the work done on time. As the crew was in place, the man with the Vitamin "D" appeared, "and the son of a bitch wouldn't leave." The team waited for two hours until sunrise. The heist was abandoned. A minimum wage milkman had cost the crew a boat load of cash. As it happened, the non-descript milkman was paid his bi-weekly wage from the company's payroll cash deposited in the very safe that was the target of Billy "O" and his band of renown. On the way back to Youngstown, the usually cool and collected Billy "O" was just that; He never said a word. Years later, when he learned of the unnatural death of his former benefactor, Joey Naples, sometime in 1992, his only thoughts returned to that Nebraska job. It was only then that Billy unleashed his anger, creating new and insightful curse words, something having to do with the milkman's mother and a Nebraska farm animal. It was for mature audiences only.

In this same category, was the legendary tale of the brown suits floating down the Mahoning River. It's always a headache when you break into a men's suit store, and find that the suits on the rack were the identical suits, minus the tags, that you had stolen a month ago. Now you had to consider stealing them yet again, and selling them back to your fence. Bill was so angry he ordered his crew to take the hundred or so suits and dump them in the local mining quarries, on the outskirts of Lowellville, Ohio.

Sometimes, even a "safe" job did not work out, and the safe was empty when the crew opened it off site. The safe had to be disposed of-and in Bill's area of the country, those same mining quarries were the place where many empty safes were buried at sea. "I had dumped so many safes into the dark waters of those mining quarries, I wondered if the fish had any room to move around!"

Nothing beats getting caught doing something bad, really bad, by your mother. Billy "O" was no exception. Early in his career, Bill's mother caught him with an unopened safe he had brought back to a place near his home. His mother, with a look that could kill even the man of steel, asked Billy, "Is this life worth it all to you, young man?" Bill didn't miss a beat. "I don't know momma; I haven't opened it yet."

Who knew?

Chapter XV

"One Small Step For Man"

"That's one small step for man, one giant leap for mankind." People of a certain age remember where they were and who they were with when Neil Armstrong uttered that one, modest historical phrase, that said all that needed to be said. Human beings, for the first time, had set foot on a celestial body other than mother earth. Kids growing up during the 1960's space race, many times referred to as NASA kids, remember all of the launches leading up to the Apollo 11 mission which landed on the moon on July 20th, 1969. The entire world, thanks to the magic of the technology developed during this space race, would be able to watch, live, on television, the first steps of Neil Armstrong, as he climbed down the lunar module ladder and set foot on the moon.

Televisions at that time, in spite of Billy "O"'s best efforts, were still an item that was not a fixture in every home in America. In fact, clearly embedded in my memory as a ten-year-old, was the scene in New York's Times square. The people of New York cramped, pushed, nudged and slid sideways, jostling each other for a position in front of a store window, where a television was playing the live broadcast of Walter Cronkite calling the play by play of the moon landing. I will always remember that back in Ohio, I was in the local music center with my father, having just completed my trumpet lessons, when live, snowy coverage of the historical event was broadcast. At approximately 4:20 p.m. E.D.T., fellow Ohio boy Neil announced to all the world, "The Eagle has landed."

The images appearing on television screens were hypnotic, compelling and spell binding. I clearly recall people, from all walks of life, being 'glued", literally, to the tube when astronaut Armstrong landed on the lunar surface. Humans stood frozen, their eyes riveted for minutes, upon the flickering tube of early black and white television sets, and if you were lucky, on the pioneering color television models. It was if one could not move, even if they wanted to or had to. The event simply demanded and commanded the complete attention of all watching.

Billy Olive and his crew were no exception. Billy was as patriotic as the next American, perhaps more. His entire family had served in World War II or Korea, with the majority of the Olive men not returning. They had given their last full measure of devotion. Bill watched the lunar landing from a television set in a bar at a hotel in some hokey small city in Pennsylvania. The crew was there on business, but were not about to miss this spellbinding event.

In the late 1960's, most hotels, large and small, offered safety deposit boxes to guests to place their valuables in while they patronized the hostel for a day, or two. This particular hotel, unlike the others, did not spread the wealth of its guests in separate locations, under different locks and keys. Instead, the mild-mannered hotel manager, working alone, would inquire each guest as to whether they have any valuables such as jewelry, cash, rings or other items that they wanted placed in the hotel safe. Billy "O" was sure of this, as he was also asked the same question by the manager of the Inn. Anything of significant value was placed in that one, nondescript safe, that was barely hidden under the cash register at the hotel restaurant and bar, where the manager could keep a close watch of it. In true fact, the manager, at all times, was not more than a half a foot away from the safe, as he recognized the importance of protecting its contents.

Police reports and gossip on the street would record, the next day, that the local manager was a man of integrity, intelligence and an employee of value to the hotel chain. Nothing in the police report indicated that the man in charge of the safe was "in on it." He was never accused of any sort of dereliction of duty. Yet the gossip continued, in search of a suspect, as the local police detective assigned to the case tried to piece together this mystery. Apparently, the safe contained quite a bit of cash and jewelry, as the morning newspaper characterized the haul as very, very significant.

The race to the moon began with a challenge from President John F. Kennedy, issued to the American people, "to place a man on the moon, and return him safely before the end of this decade." JFK called the nation to arms on this matter in early 1961, on the heels of the launch of the soviet satellite sputnik and the Russian's early manned moon flight attempts. Billions were spent the next decade on this project and now, the American public, along with all the world, was moments away from watching this adventure come to pass.

The manager at the Nowhere Inn, and I say this in a respectful way, was no exception to the thrill of it all. He, like most human beings alive on the earth at the time, had his mind and eyes and everything attached to him focused on that small snowy box, which carried live images of the greatest event in the history of mankind. As the hypnotic voice of Walter Cronkite, who himself, as he would later admit, could hardly contain both his excitement and trepidation during this lunar landing, the suspense was truly surreal. The people watching were as spellbound as the most trusted newsman in America. These images were beamed around the bar and restaurant on that eventful day. It was almost as if the humble manager of the hotel was lost in the gravity of it all, as most were, except perhaps, one man.

Billy "O" was at the top of his game in 1969. While he looked at the snowy pictures of the surface of the moon, he noticed that everyone else present at the hotel bar and restaurant were doing likewise, and this included that hotel desk clerk in charge of the safe. Billy "O" did not fail to notice that the manager was the only one in charge of shepherding this safe of safes, and mentally had noted that the metal box itself was virtually attached to the big toe of this man.

Billy and the crew were at this place of hospitality as it related to another business venture they were focused on, scheduled for later that evening. Billy, who noticed the safe hours before the moon landing, was indeed aware of the unfortunate fact that the hotel super was never more than six inches from it. He had passed upon any attempt to borrow or relocate the safe and empty its contents into the trunk of his vehicle. But for once in his life, lady luck was about to smile on the Korean Military Policeman turned master thief. For on that day, in that dreary little hole in the wall motel in backwoods Pennsylvania, the moon landing not only opened the door for mankind to travel into space, exploring all of its wonders and mysteries, but also opened the front door of this lovely hotel, allowing Billy to shuffle the safe to another crew member, as the manager's eyes stayed glued to the set.

It was later concluded, by the investigating detective, that the safe was tossed out the door and whisked away at almost the precise moment Armstrong placed his foot on lunar soil. As the network concluded the live coverage of the event, some twenty minutes later, Billy was long gone, suitcase and safe securely in tow, with the further satisfaction of seeing, at that shitty little hotel, fellow Ohio native Neil Armstrong making all of mankind's dreams come true.

Chapter XVI

A SERIES OF DREAMS

PART I

William George Olive, while sitting in the back of his shop, with scrap metal littering it's floors and hanging on nails driven into its dreary gray cement walls, drifted off into a twilight sleep of sorts, in the middle of this particular day. It was that kind of semi-conscious mental state where thoughts flow freely as the truth seeks to emerge, digging itself out from the clutter of past days.

Bill saw himself, while in this state of mind, as a young man again. Billy "O" is sitting on the railroad tracks, looking down toward the coming train, kneeling next to the tracks.

"Billy, get away from there. Go trapping, or steal some more televisions. But for God's sake, get away from that track." Pop Shraum always watched out for Billy. Billy, not paying any heed to Pop's command, ran up the hill for dinner, almost running into Pinky.

"Dance little Pinky, Dance." Bill whispered."

"Billy, why aren't you playing baseball? I love to watch you play."

"Dance away little girl, that train is coming. Tell pops to watch for the train. I am going to pick up Sun-yee." "She is waiting for me at the club. We are hitting a store tonight, you should come." "Cash and jewelry, you don't have to live like this. I will buy that house on South Main for you and the kids. This guy, I never knew he was hurting you. I would have dummied him, no questions asked. I ran this town. Look at the uniform they gave me; United States Army, Military Police!"

"It's okay Billy." Pinky, while finishing her words, began to morph into an adult Shirley. (Speaking her mature voice, with bruises on her neck and under her eyes.) "I kept it quiet.. Bill."

"I would have killed him, you know."

"What would you use, your curveball? You should have signed those papers to play Major League ball! That was a big deal, Billy."

"It wasn't enough money. They said to wait a few months and they would offer more."

"Bill, you waited fifty years, and you did get more for yourself. But it wasn't from pitching!"

"Shirley, how bad did he hurt you?"

"He is gone now Bill, it's all okay, I like living down the hall from you big brother." "Where is Bunny?"

"I think she is in Seoul, or somewhere. She knows everything about me, about you. Bill paused, and in a trance warned Pinky. "Don't go into those bars, Pinky. That's a man's hang out. These are not good guys." "They don't know how to treat a lady." Bill looked down. "I miss mom and dad."

"I saw them yesterday, Billy. I tried to talk to them, but they just stared at me, looking right through me, and walked over a hill."

"Pinky, can you find them?

"I can't now, Billy. But Bunny can. I talk to her every night."

"She is sleeping, isn't she Pinky?"

"Everyone thinks she is. But she sees everything. She's like an angel."

"Oh Billy, I saw that horse you loved, he let me pet him and I gave him a carrot and I bit half and he made that noise with his nose. He was a dream. He danced like me. He was a winner that day. He blinked at me! You can always tell a winner by the way they blink."

"You thought you lost money at the track, but you paid for him to stay there and kept him running. You loved that horse Billy; I can feel it." "He remembers you. It wasn't the money, you loved the smell of the green valley and trees around the track, the sunsets peeking over the starter's cage, the warm up laps, rooting for your favorite. You brought jellybeans with you. You had fun Billy. Fun!"

"Pinky, is momma still in her room? Seven years and she hasn't come out." " What did that Doctor say?" "Did you care for momma? She was afraid to come out of her room."

"She is in Korea, Billy, with Sun-yee and little Bill."

"Where is Olive?" Bill, looking puzzled.

"She is back at your house Bill. At home. She is getting ready to sell it. You have to go away for a while, and so does she and little Bill." "You have to go back there Billy, you have to watch little Bill when you come home."

"Billy, Pop Shrum is working alone, on the gutters at the Cahill house." (pause) "Dad is gone Bill." "Out of pain."

"That can't be!"

"Pops is still here, Billy." "He wants to go on a job with you and then to a game." "Carl Hubbell was in town asking for you. He wanted you to play football. I just laughed.", Pinky smiled.

"I'm a baseball player! Tell him Pinky!"

"No Billy, you steal stuff." Pinky morphed back into Shirley.

"Everyone has cancer here, Bill. You, and Mrs. Benoti, Dad, Pop Shraum; But he didn't know it." "But you wouldn't know it! They just smile when you ask them how they are feeling. They are different now Bill. No more suffering. I should know. I took care of all of them, remember?" Pinky asked.

"That black soldier you shot, back in South Korea, is with Mom and Dad. I can't make out what they are talking about." "No, wait! I think he is asking for you." "He wanted to come to that ceremony with Mom and Dad. They are giving you a big award for stealing all that stuff and never getting caught."

"No Pinky, it's for baseball." Bill snapped back.

"Don't take young Bill, Pinky. Please, don't take him there, unless it's for Baseball."

"If that's what you want Bill."

"Billy, young Bill won't go either way. He said his chest hurts. He is staying in Campbell with Olive." "Hey, I fixed dancin' Hank up with that gal... how about that!" "Bunnie tells me they are getting married!"

Pinky dances, and twirls and sings by the railroad tracks. The dream floats on.

"Get out of there Pinky! "Those trains are coming!" "Get Pops out of there too!"

Billy is shouting as loud as he could, but no one can hear his voice; It was like trying to talk underwater.

"Pops, come on. They have two, two today. I am sure..coming one after another." "Get away from the tracks." "Pinky, dance away and Pops will follow you. Tell him you're a little blue bird. He always liked bluebirds."

The story of Pinky was heartbreaking. At four foot, five inches, she was an attractive young Italian girl that would place her small, but fiery frame and heated rhetoric, between those that could not speak for themselves, or defend against the classic classroom bullies. Whether breaking up an unfair fight on the back of a high school staircase by twisting her tiny frame, like a piece of copper, between two combatants, or using some other clever means, you could be sure that Pinky, Shirly Olive herself, now a person known of her own accord around town, would not let a scintilla of injustice go on in her beloved hometown.

In the ensuing years, after her father died of cancer, Shirley cared for tens or perhaps hundreds of cancer victims, with a hospice of sorts, dancing and singing to bring cheer to their last days. She was mother Teresa before it was fashionable. The energy of that little flower did not wane a bit. Through the trial and tribulations of two wars, the assassination of her beloved John F. Kennedy and the horrifying deaths of Dr. King, and Robert F Kennedy, she just kept dancing. As time, social custom and changing historical events provided the canvas upon which her life would be etched, Shirley remained a constant servant to the people of her small town.

Shirley, "Pinky" Olive, would later, as the time approached, marry a man. Her compassion and desire to help people was now to be put to the ultimate test. Her new husband was a bit of a pathetic character, but that is what attracted her. She wanted to fix him. After a fairly brief courtship, she married this man and had two beautiful children, starting a family of their own. As the wheels of the universe turn in this awesome mysterious creation, its rules of fairness are difficult to understand. Bad men prevail, good men fall. Women are placed in situations that either are a test of their faith, or a cruel hoax; Betting on the wrong roulette color, sometimes landing on black, sometimes on red, it was all a wager. The roulette wheel, in the case of her marriage, landed on the wrong color. It made one wonder, "Is the creator of this game a hoaxster or an infinite being of cosmic love?" Some believed he was both.

Pinky, the dancing little pixie, the little twirling girl of the town, married a psychotic monster, mental illness bringing him and her two small children to places evil spirits dare tread; Pinky and her children were now held hostage by this devil.

They lived in a place called hell. These were the days that Shirly never spoke about. These were the days that would shock the conscience of any person claiming to be human, if only they saw the sadistic happenings transpiring behind her bolted front door. Who or what force would dare torture the little girl who defended the weak, cared for the sick, cheered her brother on, or provided hospice for the dying?" " Was her husband truly a mentally ill man, as many now opine that he was, or was it the evil caught up inside him that caused his outward appearance of mental disability?" The brutality and hopelessness of it all, the lack of an escape route, and the fear of speaking out to friends and family made Shirley "Pinky" Olive a prisoner in her own home. In the end, Pinky managed to escape, taking her two young children with only the clothes on their backs, fleeing their home which had been turned into a dungeon of destruction. People who came to learn the truth of the affair murmured,

" God himself must have intervened in that household, providing temporary grace for those two children who witnessed, and were victimized, by the horror of all that went on."

Her brother, Billy "O", a benefactor of skills from his mentor, a man who shall remain nameless, but who rivaled the Dickens character Jack Dawkins, (known as the "Artful Dodger"), was, in spite of his immaculate training, no more the wise. If it were not so, the local quarries would, no doubt, be filled with another safe or two, containing body parts. Yet, this spouse from another dimension, who had no earthly or heavenly reason to be in her life, choking her within an inch of her death each day, planting the seeds that would cause ruin later in the adult lives of their children, would one day vanish to parts unknown.

A new life had begun in the autumnal equinox of her years, but her spirit, in spite of it all, never was quenched or extinguished, never injured or lobotomized. It was as keen as ever- even if the lord had mistakenly, if only for a bit, turned his back on her and her children. Pinky would now be able to walk further down the path of her life, working three jobs, regaining her footing in the community, and continuing her hospice care, giving comfort and solace to those around her. She continued giving love and service to others, while she, out of necessity, worked odd jobs and other commitments in order to support her children after their apocalypse.

After all that she had been through, two less told stories out of hundreds, represented her qualifications to be nominated for sainthood. She gave her only worldly possession she loved, a somewhat damaged bicycle, to a young girl who wanted more than anything to ride one. That she did. The second legendary tale was transferred from God's ear to only those who were worthy of hearing it. In the times her children had no food or place to lay their damaged bodies and minds, on a comforting bed that could bury the horrors they endured while watching their mother tortured day each day, Pinky took to work at one of the less than elegant places that catered to men who were in need of a shave and who had liquor on their breathe from a week's worth of hooching. She had to serve them their poison, and under the direct supervision of her boss, Pinky's main duty was to smile when roaming hands found their way to places on a woman's body they were not entitled to be. Yet she smiled, when remembering how she taught a middle-aged man named Hank, shy in his own interesting way, how to dance. Smiling' Hank eventually found and did indeed marry the love of his life, all because Pinky taught him how to dance. Years later, Hank came back and thanked Shirley Olive for giving him that courage and talent. Pinky, as always, put herself last her entire life, and it was equally clear that in the end, she would be placed first at the right hand of God.

As I was reminiscing with Billy "O" one afternoon, I mentioned just one word, "Pinky". The look on Bill's face told me all I needed to know. It was the first, but not the last time that Billy came to a point of showing emotion. The look, that squint of his sharp eyes and the slow lowering of his his head as he stared down at the ground told me that yes, he knew the hell his sister had endured, but was powerless at the time to change the course of her life due to his own destiny which separated them by time and circumstance. This realization, almost more than any other, crushed his very soul.

Chapter XVII

SERIES OF DREAMS

PART II

Ted walked in on Billy snoring. It was around noon, when Bill awoke.

"Let's head down and get you a set of wheels, Bill. You need to get around. We can stop at the restaurant for lunch." "What the hell is going on, you were snoring like a bear." (laughter). Billy and Ted, the saint assigned to him by God, went to see about that car, and ended up buying it. Billy "O" insisted on driving. He was 90 years old; Big deal, he drove better than most of these kids who are on those damned i-phones while driving.

"Jellybeans and Richie are waiting down there for us. She made the special for ya." That was enough to get Billy moving. Once he was out of that chair, he moved, still having the swagger that persuaded those ladies to help him put the stolen furs he dropped, taken from a nearby J.C. Penny's store in an unnamed City in upper state New

York, back safely into his arms. "Is Jellybeans in one of her moods," Bill laughs. "She is in rare form. God must really love Richie!"

Billy Olive felt renewed from his morning siesta. It was later that afternoon that this five-star Lowellville treasure rolled out its Italian special. It was heavenly. The Italian people always met on Sundays at mom's house, the extended family together, for a home cooked meal of pasta, brazouli, (steak), homemade sauce and meatballs. Billy "O" and Ted were hungry after being jerked around by automobile sales-men most of the afternoon. They were now indeed, at the right place.

I remember reading somewhere that when you eat a big, heavy meal, you always, like a big bear, want to take a long nap. I recall the Christmas Eve Italian feasts when all the men would eat, then head for their favorite couches as the women cleaned the table and did the dishes. It was a different time. Years later, and I can't remember when, I read that the stomach required a large supply of blood to digest all the food, and the head, without proper circulation and a short blood supply, produced that drowsy feeling that leads to sleep. No matter the exactitude of the scientific explanation, Billy, after this awesome meal, was indeed a bit drowsy, and Ted, not wanting to take a chance with Bill's condition, drove him home. Billy crawled up into his bed, and put on a cozy paisley blanket. Ted slowly closed the door so as not to make Bill hear the squeaky hinges, shut the light and left for the evening. It was about six or six thirty p.m. by this time. Much like a doctor administering an anesthetic, the pasta indeed did Bill in, putting him into a deep, deep sleep, in the arms of that blanket and up under the protection of that grand apartment he had called home for many of his golden years.

Fast asleep, now much like Joseph in the Bible, Billy dreamed a deep dream. His dream took him down a brown dirt path high up in the wooded hills of his youth. He loved checking those traps for critters and counting things he caught, and the ones that got away. He walked, sometimes slowing down, slightly bending over and stretching his frame, looking for something deep within the woods which he could not find. After a time, the green shade which he loved so much, the smell and virginity of it all, abruptly ended. He found himself in a deep valley, surrounded by nothing but mountains of rocks.

The West wall of the valley was lined with mile high jagged climbing rocks, the East Side with dirt and rocky trails, with most of them being long and winding passages up the mountainous hills. The Northern cliff, almost forty-five degrees on an angle, looked virtually impossible to negotiate. There would be no climbing up that hillside. Toward the South, an equally steep labyrinth of rocks and uneven hills with brush and thorns, led to a god-like block of gray granite, with men of valor riding upon magnificent horses. It beckoned Bill to come toward it. It called out to him to heed its challenge.

Bill dreamed in technicolor, like most humans. When he found himself on rock island, with no place to go but up, he let out a rebel yell, waiting around for a reply by echo. Now I am no physics professor, but when in that position amongst a vortex of stone, sound does reflect, and bounce back. Alone, but not panicking, and he never did, young Bill would take stock of the challenge. At 18 years old, he was in terrific shape. Billy considered his options. He had two. He could try to climb out of the canyon, or stand there and die. Hobson was laughing somewhere. Not much on these kinds of choices, young William took advantage of his youth and began to climb. He tried the Southern route, toward the images. It was built for him. "This isn't so bad, it's kind of beautiful, in a way." As young Bill picked up the pace, with silence still ruling the valley, he made great progress. After a time, Bill decided to take a break. He had travelled a good distance but time, he discovered, began to be a problem. With each step he took, Billy Olive was aging.

Billy stood back up and continued, with hand over hand climbing and foot spiking, moving like a spider, climbing up the walls of a crooked house. After what seemed about an hour, Bill stopped for another break. After resuming his quest, the short break now long ago in his memory, Bill, for reasons unknown to him at the time, began to "get winded." After cutting his hand on a rock, Bill looked down at his wrist and lower arm. It was no longer the smooth, muscular skin of a young man playing baseball in the springtime back in Lowellville. His skin was aging, getting taught and tithe a bit. After the sun began to set, Bill noticed a weakness in one of his arms. Bill's left arm, which was used to pitch his Lowellville looper, the one injured permanently in a game when he came back from the war, was weak, making it virtually impossible for him to hold onto the rocks with both arms and hands. He slipped once or twice courtesy of the weakness of that arm. He decided to sit a bit on the most stable rock in the area, resting his injured arm, while he came up with a plan to climb up the rest of the way.

After a few blows of air, Bill began to think about what he would have to do to survive the night. Suddenly, without warning, Billy heard the sound of his mother's voice. "Billy, come down from there, it's time to eat." Billy "O" instinctively jumped to his feet and began the final climb to the top of somewhere. After what seemed like weeks, Bill was ready to stop, surrender, give in-something so foreign to him that the heavens above had trouble reconciling this decision with the creature they had magnificently made. At the same instant, Bill felt a hand touch his injured arm. He whisked around, out of reflex, and was almost shocked, definitely bewildered by what he observed.

"You could have shot me with your M15 rifle, right through the heart, in the bar that night." " I was a black man, in a white man's army, and I took a broken bottle to your throat. But you didn't kill me. You winged me and took me to the hospital."

"Hold on to my uniform." Within a blink of time in the mind's eye, Billy was at the top of Stone Mountain. He turned to thank the soldier he shot in Korea. As he glanced back to grab his uniform with his left arm, the first class private, United States Army, blacker than night, disappeared. Bill heard an echo. He looked down toward where he thought it came from. "I am down here at the bottom. I have my own mountain to climb too." Billy was half in awe and half amused. "Was that you I saw at the top all this time?" "Why in the hell didn't you come up here earlier and help me. Anyway, thanks pal, I mean private, I couldn't have made those last two miles." "I owed you one, M.P., and you won't hear that every day." Bill, for some unusual reason, was not overly impressed. He was more interested in how the private made the canyon mountain produce an echo. It was one more surreal thing he accepted, but couldn't explain.

William George Olive was at the top of the mountain. "What the hell are you guys doing here." "What do you mean? You ok bill? We are hitting Loblaws and Penny's tonight. You drinking today Bill?" "Now those new heavy, heavy steel safes have a problem. You can't lift them with a short crane onto a truck, and they have thick iron and steel coverings. You can't peel the layers away. But, their locks are shit!" You could almost turn and open them with a pair of pliers or even your hands. Just open the top and grab the money bags. Unbelievable." "Billy, who is the young kid with us?" "Where?" "He is in the back of that beater Chevy we have, going back to the house in Struthers." " Come on. You're pulling my chain." "Go see for yourself."

Bill walked toward the car door, and with some hesitation, looked inside. He had to cross an entire baseball field to get there. "Olive, what the hell are you doing here. Is that young Bill?" " Why did you bring him here, you know better?" Young Bill was in his baby bassinet. "I don't want this for the boy!" "He can't do this kind of thing. It's too damned dangerous." "Don't make matters worse. Get out of the front seat and I will get someone to drive you and the baby home." Billy "O" looked behind him for an instant, as he was trained to do. When he turned back around, Olive and his young son were gone. "Billy, come on, we are ready to go. It's clear. Let's get the shit and get out of here." "I can't leave now. These people are watching a good ballgame. I think I am pitching and the bases are loaded. My father Dominic and Grandpa and my sisters are watching me. This is for all the marbles guys. We needed to win and there were pro scouts watching me." "This is big time. The Lawrence County league." "I have played against grown men since I was fourteen."

Billy looked out at the baseball field as the crew began to leave. Benny whispered, "Billy, finish your game. This is where you pitch that no hitter. I saw the box score. Bring it home for the boys and everyone. We have your share. You can pick it up back in Struthers, I will make sure the baby and Olive make it home." It was almost as if Benny was like his head coach making a trip to the mound in this tense situation. Maybe he was. At any rate, Billy struck out the last hitter. After a mild celebration, he went back to the clubhouse, showered and climbed into a 1947 Plymouth and drove back to Lowellville. A crowd of people, led by Pinky, cheered wildly for Bill. But there were unborn F.B.I. agents watching in the background. It was time for Bill to get back to the shop and finish weighing his scrap metal. He was trying to wake up, but he could not. He was trapped in a dream of his own making.

Chapter XVIII

THE VISITOR

It was almost midnight. Billy "O" had been sleeping for six hours. He rustled around a bit, awoke, took a quick look about, and went back to sleep. Billy returned to the land of sweet dreams and horrific nightmares; The roll of the dice determined which would be playing on the first bill.

Billy never, ever wanted young Bill to be a part of his weekend business. This thought drove his dreams this night. Deep in sleep, he has a night terror. Billy is screaming at Sun-yee and Olive that he never wanted this for his son, and that in his world, for one reason and a few others, it wasn't safe. To be on Billy's crew, you needed to come from a certain time, have a certain way you looked at the world, be quick on your feet and able to fit in like a part of a well-oiled machine. Billy "O"'s machine had been working with great success for quite some time. Young Bill would not be able to fit in as fast as needed. The events of the year, with a change of address and short stay in a government boarding house, left Billy with a full schedule to complete. He would not have time to mentor young Bill.

The senior living home in Lowellville, while active during the day, was now quiet; It's a perfect stage for weird dreams and the surfacing of the unsaid.

Bunny was sitting at the edge of the bed where Bill lay with his eyes closed.

"You know Bunny, he can't do this stuff."

"Bill, I know there is more. It's a fear. What happened?"

"Well it would have never happened to him. He's too smart to do anything that will harm him. He doesn't have the heart of a thief."

"Who was the smart one Bill? Young Bill did the right thing, he worked for Pop Shraum's company, sometimes with you, sometimes without you. Pops loves him for that."

"Bunny, sometimes a fella, or a young guy fits into this life. You try to help him "learn" the business. He smells the money." " Then, before you know it, he thinks he can do better. He gets addicted to the money. Give me more, more, more!"

"You mean like you big brother?"

"I could never fool you Bunny. You were always smarter. Some of these guys from the outfit, I called them 'dumb and dumber', got themselves killed. They thought they could do what we did by themselves. Twenty-nine of them. Greedy. All dead."

"Bill, that's not what I am talking about, and you know that."

"There was this kid, he had everything going for him, he was from the neighborhood. He didn't need this kind of work. He was a baseball player like me. But it wasn't enough. He had nothing growing up. We tried to help his family. I brought him on the crew."

"Where is he now Bill?"

"When he came on board, it was as if he took his athletic talent and used it to become a great heist man, a real burglar. He could run fast, quiet, he had strength to climb fences and walls, he blended in and he was a strong kid, no one to mess with."

"Bill, he sounds like someone I know. You should have discouraged him."

"Bunnie, you don't get it. Once you see the money, how easy we made it, how easy I made it, the greed, it ruins you. Nothing was enough for the kid. He always wanted more!"

"Where is he now, Bill? It's me, Bunny, you can tell me anything. I am alone in here."

"The kid goes out on his own, goes over to New York; He liked diamonds and coins. He did great, so I hear, even started a crew for himself. I liked the kid. He reminded me of...but the kid had big eyes. He thought he could get over on anyone. He didn't care who he gamed or thumped. But these New York people, they had rules. I never would double cross them or try to take what isn't mine or take their share. They had rules, Bunny."

"Billy, I taught school for many, many years. I know all about rules. Some rules you just cannot break. There are severe consequences. I expelled many students in my day. Other rules Bill, you know, a slap on the wrist and you get a warning and a second chance.

"Did this kid get a second chance Bill?"

"Bunny, the rule he broke-there are no second chances. You don't bite the hand that feeds you; And he did."

"He's gone Bunny, gone. I should have seen that one coming. But I didn't Bunny, and now this young man, ..I should have said no, when he came to me."

"It could have happened to anyone."

"Someone like young Bill Jr.?"

"Yeah Bunny, my biggest fear. I would never forgive myself."

"But you protected him, Billy. You picked him up every day for the real family business, helping people."

"Bunny, I think about that kid every day."

"Who, the one like you Bill, the greedy good time Charlie one?"

"No, my son, Bill. It could easily have been him Bunny, just a matter of the roll of the dice; Just like life. It's all a matter of chance."

Chapter XIX

"NOTES FROM A HEIST"

Watch the front door. Count how many people walk in every five minutes. When is the busiest time and day for the store? Is there an alarm system? How many police cars are in the neighborhood? I need to move to a closer location. I will walk by but only once, from a distance. Maybe I should have brought my camper on this one, just parked it up the street a bit, and hunker down to watch.

I see one main road in front of the store, a small-town square, mostly people minding their own business. Two roads, one on each side of the building; Looks like a back entrance for the delivery trucks. The one side doesn't have any lights. They must be using that for daytime drops. The other side has some lighting. Will check tonight. What is the quickest way out of this town? The state route is two blocks away. This could be the best exit route. Let me watch one of their tractor trailers bring the inventory into the back door. How long does it take for him to squeeze through? Is the exit alley, on the other side, bigger, or smaller? Look, it takes him longer. Note that.

Back to people count. It's busier at noon and at five. Is there a security guard after hours? I will take a walk tonight, go down the street for ice cream or something. Remember to tell Benny.

It's been two and a half days. I saw eighty people go in, and sixty people come out with purchases. They have top of the line clothing. Women's wear. I am guessing their take for the week is substantial. When does the brinks truck come to pick up their money? How long do they keep it locked up? I need to find someone who worked there as a clerk. Reminder to ask around. How many trips would the four of us have to take to load the truck? How long from the clothing racks to the back of the store? Can we carry them off the rack, or are there boxes of inventory? If we have to hit the ground, is there a side door to rumble. What is the average cost? Look in the newspapers. See if a sale is on, or not. Calculate the gross receipts. Do they take cash, yes, this is a cash town, lots of cash. Big article in the paper about holiday dresses on sale. Must have marked them up really high, now cutting back for regular sale. When are the boys coming in? Wait, some shield just walked in. Is it near closing time? Look, he walked out with a box, never paid. How about that?

The boys have to wear gloves, tight black gloves. Three hauling the inventory off the racks and one at the lookout point. There are a few people hanging out in front of the store at night. The lookout has to use a silver dollar to tap on the front window if the law comes around. Who is with the crew? Ah shit. That New York guy who got caught falling through a ceiling. I am tired of carrying their people. Use him as a mule, let him carry the load. Benny and I will direct the traffic inside. Find the best way to go from point A. to point B.. Stay away from the front window, stay low. If the tins flash their lights into the front store window, hit the ground, on your stomach, and crawl along the carpet. Stay down. Street lights just about reflect off the front window. Whoever designed the building should have made them put the lights closer.

Ok, Benny, you stay here, you two get rooms at the Holiday Suites down the street. One the upper floor, one the lower floor. Stay separate from each other while you are walking around the hotel and the lounge. You have to act like complete strangers. We enter from the back inventory door. Note to Joe; The truck is at the towing company, three blocks away. They have both Pa. and Ohio plates for you. You know when to switch. The night watchman comes around every hour, probably a retired railroader. Wait till about 2:00 am. He will be off his game a bit by then. He starts at 7:00 p.m. or 8:00 p.m. Now, go in the second driveway. Take a walk down that way, put a hat on, big brim, dress up, and walk by. There are no lights. You can't hit the building. Measure it up. Come around and to the back. I got a tip the back door has an easy lock; I will punch it and turn the pin. We rumble in, take 'em off the rack and rumble back. You gotta watch coming out. You can't turn around and go the way you came. There ain't no room. You have to keep going, pull around the other side road. It has lights. Cut the delayed alarm wires while we are inside. Go slow on the way out. No noise. People are sleeping next door. Take a left, go toward the towing yard, one mile West, and get on the freeway, no turnpike. We don't have our toll man again, tonight. Don't forget, stay on the freeway, no tolls! Jimmy, there has to be boxes of shirts. Let's get the suits and shirts. Forget the dresses. They are too big, it's like a holiday dress or something, not like Bobby Brooks stuff. The truck is big enough, we could take it all. Don't touch the mannequins.

Can we make a chain, just hand the suits down the line to each other? Less body movement. But we would have to stand the whole time. They had one search light since I was here, at around 1 a.m. Can't change it. Ok, no booze. We go in around 2 a.m., and have wheels on the ground, leaving before 2:45 a.m. If we get squeezed, take them on a chase toward the towing yard. We will break the other way. There is a car behind the hotel I am in. Come back and pick us up in that park over there. The third entrance. Listen to your scanners. These guys chat a lot.

We meet in Struthers, by way of Lowellville. Use the backroad, Wilson Ave. in Cambell, but drop off the truck at Danny's in Lowellville, behind the barn. Take Wilson Ave. from Campbell and go the back way. No lights. If some cruiser stops you, we got it covered. Use the code word. Last note; burn the notes.

Wilson Ave. was the backroad into Lowellville, beginning in Campbell, Ohio, just over one of the main bridges connecting it to steel town. On the right side of the snake twisted road were rows and rows of shadow covered steel mill buildings, entrances for workers, and side roads for large equipment that someone would drive into the dark, mysterious corners of the steel plants. The skies near the road were lit in neon hues of purple, yellow, white and black smoke, creating surreal illusions against the sky; A poor man's version of the northern lights. On the left side of the tracks, equally high, was a mile long row of trees, protruding from the brick roads of the high hills of Campbell, houses hidden in between. This secret roadway snaked its way, silent and gray, blending into the scenery. During the day, the road was visible. At night, it disappeared, only lit up by the headlights of an occasional automobile travelling in the opposite direction. On this night, there would be no headlights. Black ruled the night and the midnight cargo of Billy "O"'s crew arrived without notice, on a ghost train, invisible to the naked eye of any honest law man who may have been on patrol in the area, and there were only a few in this town.

Before dawn, the crew was back safely in Lowellville and nearby Struthers. The haul for the day was unloaded and stored, stuffed into a house in Struthers. The open air market went into operation the same day. Policemen, lawyers and Judges had put orders in ahead of time. A suit for Judge Pinnozza, a stylish hat for the good counselor. The prosecutor, in a nearby suburb of Warren, Ohio, requested a pin striped black suit with an off white shirt and red tie. Mill workers had more cash. They wanted suits for church and one good fella needed an outfit for his brother- in laws funeral. By lunchtime, the haul was gone, sold American. No questions. No investigations. No problems. It's like that when you're on a roll. You can do no wrong.

In William George Olive's case, this roll would continue for forty years. If there was a trophy for "Best heist in a season", they would win it every year. Their precision and good luck almost made the contest unfair. They counted the money then gambled it away, the curse of winning was the cost of their success.

Chapter XX

THE VISITOR REDUX

"You know Billy, you were always the happiest when you were trapping those critters back in the woods, up behind Bellino's farm and back up the hills. You loved going up the next day to see what you snarred."

"Bunny, I was a kid back then, things change."

"But Dad knew you like a book. He told me once that trapping was your heaven, you liked to be alone; And on the pitcher's mound. You were alone there too."

"I liked the game, Bunny. I was pretty good, but so were the other guys."

"But you turned down that contract to play with the Giants, how could you!" " It wasn't enough?" " You always wanted more."

"I saw you in that New York job, or "heist" as they called them back in those times. How did you get into that jewelry store?" " You must have made a lot of girls happy."

"No Bunny, we sold the stuff to a fence. We made a ton of money, a ton."

"But where is Bill Jr.?"

"I have a confession to make. You know the money Momma and Papa were saving for you, for college? I had to "borrow" some of it. They didn't know. I'm 90 years old Bunny, and I am sorry; I know it was wrong."

"You disappointed them Bill. But I forgive you, I still made it to college. You know that."

"Billy, why are you volunteering for that war, over in Korea? Don't go, Bill. Pops needs you at home."

"Everyone is volunteering Bunny. I have too."

"Billy, you could have killed that sailor, shot him in the heart, but you only hit him in the leg; Like some of those critters that you trapped, and then let go."

"No, I skinned a lot of them, I think."

"I have been looking around for you Bill. Where have you been all these years?"

"I had the wife and kids, you know."

"But you liked that money Bill, you must have gambled it all away. All those heists, and look, you are broke, or are you?"

"I get by. I live in the same building as Pinky."

"Pinky is a Doll, Bill!" " I miss her. She suffered so much; you know. Or did you?" "He beat her Bill, he choked her. Your nieces and nephews grew up in a living nightmare. When was the last time you saw them?"

"I can't remember."

"Why did you let that go on?"

"I was busy, or maybe I didn't want to get involved, I don't know."

"She was your little sister Bill, how could you?"

"God damned it, quit judging me! If I knew, you know what would have happened to him. You know me Bunny."

"But you didn't have time for her Bill. But you had time to become a master at something that wasn't good, and a failure at doing something that was good."

"Like what? You don't know what I did. It was small stuff anyway."

"Billy Olive, I have seen these things! I see them now. Hundreds of televisions in Pittsburgh, hundreds of suits in Beaver Falls. You stole enough clothes to start your own women's retail chain. You emptied the shelves of shirts and socks, womens' daily wear, Italian shoes, Italian suits, men's watches, women's jewelry, ties of all colors, anything not nailed down, in half of Western Pa. (Altoona, Latrobe, Pottsdale and even New Castle). I liked some of those clothes! But you never brought me any."

"You're too honest Bunny, you probably wouldn't have taken them anyway."

"How would you know." " I really liked those dresses, Bill!"

"Yeah, if you say so. You were the honest one, the smart one. You went to College. I lost track of you after that."

"It seems like a long time ago, but here, time is not what you think it is. It is all still happening. The things we do are played over and over again. I can't seem to move on."

"You know what I am thinking about now, and I have to admit, it's funny for the old school teacher that I am-the time your boys went on that big liquor store heist, you had to rumble. The one in upstate New York."

"We were smart about that. When we rumbled, we would stay in the area, and wherever there was a broken tree branch blocking the road, we knew it was our driver who put it there. That was the signal. We would remove the branch and sure enough, he would pull up and we would jump in the back seat. Worked every time we needed rescued."

"But what if there was a bad storm, Bill, and there were hundreds of branches down? You would have had to walk twenty-five miles along the railroad tracks just to get back home!"

"I loved those tracks, everything about our town, Bunny. I miss Dad and Pops." "Bunny, he suffered so much. I am glad he didn't see me doing my weekend jobs."

"He knows Bill. He knows all about it, about you."

"How do you…"

"Just believe me Bill, he knows, and he still loves you. Same with Papa Shraum."

"I should have been there for Pops that day, I let him down."

"Those two trains Bill, one after another, no one could see the second train coming. It happened so fast. Pops tripped and fell. That was a long time ago. He doesn't want you blaming yourself anymore." (pause) Bill became silent.

"Have you seen young Bill Jr.?"

"Dad and Pops were busting at their buttons when the guys gave you that Baseball award; Back in 1994, or around that time." "They were so proud of you, Bill."

"But Pops and Dad were gone long before that. They were gone by then. I have the program, it was 1994!"

"They saw you accept the plaque and shed a tear when you made that short speech. You were the best, big brother, I remember.. a legend."

"You know Bunny, our crew rumbled for forty years, maybe more, and we never got caught."

"Bill, be honest, you did seventeen months in prison, Olive divorced you and she and young Bill had to move to another place. That was horrible, they were never the same after that."

"It was that son of bitch Frankie Benzonoti. He was a no-good snitch. We rumbled after a security guard came. We were running through a field of manure, he fell, they grabbed him. The smell was awful. He dropped a dime on me, that's the only way I did one day in the joint, Bunny."

"Listen to you, William George Olive, you talk like a thief, a no good criminal!"

"That's the point Bunny, I am; Or was. It's lonely now. My friends are all gone."

"But in those days, I was the best. Believe me Bunny. One time we were in a resort town, you would have liked it, cars had fifteen different license plates, all out of state "monied" people. We dropped in on a store they had for the rich bunch. Benny smashed into a glass case and knocked over a bunch of expensive stuff. A real bull in a China shop. Jewelry, gold bracelets, coins, we took it all. I made a bracelet, eighteen carat gold, with a two-and-a-half-inch band!" " I gave it to Olive."

"I know Bill, but she thought it was too much of a show. She put up with that life, but she had her limits."

"Yeah, we had a good marriage, I think."

"Bill, you were never there for them!"

"I had a living to make."

"Stealing and Gambling isn't much of a living." "You gave your money to those one armed bandits, at those damned casinos!" " You were never there for Olive and young Bill!"

"How did you know about that bracelet, Bunny. Only two or three people know about that?"

"I see everything here, Bill." " Your best job was the New York Diamond thing, or heist; My God, now I feel like one of your crew! You made tens of thousands of dollars on that one and split it with those thugs on that job. That was always your rule, right?"

"I made a lot of good friends in New York City on that one."

"You made some good friends?" "But Bill, they were only associates or acquitenances. They fenced property for you and made a bunch of money too."

"No Bunny, they would have done anything for me."

"Billy, a friend is for life, an acquaintance is someone who is around only while the money lasts."

"These people were not your friends. Think about it, that was a million dollar take. I can do the math. I teach it!" "That's about ten million bucks today, Bill, and after all that, none of them are around."

"But I am 90 years old for Christ's sake, Bunny."

"Bill, they were gone weeks after the gig was over, don't tell me big brother."

"You don't know what you're talking about. We took anything we wanted. We took care of our people. Our crew was razor sharp. I was proud of that. We stole beef right off the sandwiches of Arby's, you know they started in Youngstown, right? I robbed a safe at a race track in New Jersey or somewhere on the east coast, lost it all the same day, couldn't find my leather coat, and just drove up the street and "took" another one, from a top men's store. I had poker games and football pools going 24/7. We had a no limit game, Bunny, at some guy's place in Struthers. The entire day shift at the Sheet and Tube Mill would punch out on the time clock, start rotating seats, and money would roll in non-stop. The game started at 4:00 p.m. on Friday and ended Sunday at noon. We made more money on those weekends; Hell, the Mill should have just given their paychecks directly to us!"

"Billy, what about their wives and kids? These are working men, and you took their money. Their kids had no clothes, the wives had no husband for days at a time and on Monday, when school started, their children didn't have lunch money. They were ashamed! Do you know what that does to a young boy or girl?" "The funny thing is, you turned out just like them; Broke, away from home and gambling away what you 'earned.'"

"I know, Bunny, I am a degenerate gambler. I did the same thing, over and over, my entire life."

"That's not the brother I knew."

"Bunny, everyone was in on that life. Remember Chief Mancusso? His cut was ten percent off the top!" "All the mayors, councilmen, half of the police force in the county, were my customers. I must have sold them a thousand suits one year. I did what I had to do…"

"You could have earned money the honest way, but it was too hard for you big brother." "But no, you had to be the big shot!"

"Why should I do it the hard way?"

"Dad and Pops taught you morals, values, how to act like a real man. You would have been fine with the Shraum family business. It had a good name because of Pops and Dad. You could have helped people and still made an honest living. But for some reason, you went the other way."

"You're eighty-six years old Bunny, for God's sake, and in a coma! Your mind is gone, so don't lecture me."

"Maybe you're asleep Bill, maybe this is a dream, or maybe you crossed."

"No, not yet, Bunny. I have some things I need to do. A lot of people need help. I like my life now. I like my life, and I try to help a lot of people." "But if I just had another chance, a fresh start."

"How are you going to help anybody when you can't even take care of yourself!"

"It wasn't alway like that Bunny; And I know things, I know how people are. I earned my street degree. When people are in trouble, they end up at my scrap metal shop. Yeah, back there in my crappy little office. But I know how to help them Bunny, and I care about them. It wasn't like that.. for a long time."

"Like after Bill Jr...?"

"Yeah, if you say so."

"You have a good heart Billy. You just got lost somewhere, maybe in Korea. I knew about Sun-yee; And I know you're a good man. You didn't have to take in those Korean families."

"It was war time; they couldn't take care of themselves, no farm-ing...it was like hell. Seoul disappeared. They were going to die if I didn't help them."

"That's my point Billy, you did the right thing, that's the brother I knew."

"I have to go now Bill, I have to see mom."

"How is she?"

"Perfect. We are all perfect here, Billy."

"Is young Bill Jr., (pause) with you?"

"Yes Bill, and he is perfect too."

Chapter XXI

JELLY BEANS

H e would call her jelly beans, and she would just call him Billy. In any other lifetime, or two, they never would have met, yet alone become fast friends. Of a different generation, in 1985 or so, Jelly beans was lost, and Billy found her. They became Bonnie and Clyde in a short time and in that little space. She tracked him down, looking for a pair of jeans. By this time, Billy had slowed a bit, giving up safe robberies and warehouse heists for the simpler things in life, like football pools and fencing blue jeans. Jelly beans was upside down, shaken but not stirred, trying to find her way after High School. She was like an energy bunny in those days, couldn't stop talking, couldn't stop fidgeting. She was straight outta of a bad home situation and was just looking for a pair of jeans; she found the fenced jeans, at a great price too, but she found something else, a lifelong friend. That can only happen in Lowellville, Ohio.

The little booking operation that Billy put together for football games and other games of chance was humble, in both location and decor, but it began to grow. It had six phone lines and an official place of operation, and as all good operations of that nature, it made money. Any decent beginner in the life of a bookie knows you have to have a good "runner", someone you could trust to pick up the cash placed on the bets of the week, someone who was ambitious, yet not so much as to steal more than you expected. "Billy, I need some blue jeans." "Jellybeans, go pick up that money, hurry before the wire closes." And it was rumored that she did, and never stole a dime. Her career goals, whatever she dreamed of, were put on hold. She needed the mentoring of Billy Olive, and he needed a trusted partner. Gone were the days of glory, the diamonds, the jewelry, the men's suits, the women's designer apparel and the easy cold cash with dead presidents on its face, just waiting for a suitor to take them out of their iron and steel box. Now, instead of warehouses of suits, the concerns were much more limited, or to be a bit more kind, "focused." The smack talking in this crew of two never involved safes and television hauls, but instead were more like, "Do you think the Browns will win by seven?" "Where are the betting slips from last week?"

The new Butch Cassidy and Sundance gal made some noise. Raids and busted down doors became a routine thing. The Federal people needed high profile gambling busts every five years or so; It was good for their budget requests on Capitol Hill. The tales of their booking operation became well known in the town by the railroad tracks and the river. The steel mills had been long closed, but the new kids in town provided a new kind of thing to hold the town's attention; Billy and Jellybeans, live and on stage on any given Sunday. It was a time to remember.

Chapter XXII

THE LEGEND

B aseball town U.S.A.'s Old Timer's Association had a hall of
fame induction ceremony in Youngstown, Ohio, sometime
in 1994. People in the know, the scouts, coaches, players and
television booth people, who really, really know baseball, all agreed
that the Youngstown, Ohio, area, for its average size, had produced
some of the greatest athletes at the amateur and professional level of
all time. It's just the plain truth. If the peaking of the new immigrant
populations had been timed differently, or if the two world wars and
the Korean war had not produced a single shot, many of the professional names playing the game of baseball during the 1950's-1970's,
would, beyond the doubt of the people that know the game, include
a great many people from Northeastern, Ohio. One would be a left-
handed pitcher from Lowellville, Ohio. The left hander played organized amateur baseball since he was fourteen, in a league with former
major league players. It is an absolute fact that this young kid was
offered a professional contract with the New York Giants, by Carl

Hubble himself. If Carl saw something in the boy, then he had "that something" that very few people possessed; Gifted talent.

These athletes from the Youngstown area were not completely forgotten. Several respected organizations were formed and maintained which honored their own hall of fame baseball players from their hometowns, the ones that could have, should have, but for reasons of patriotism and happenstance, spent their best years playing semi-professional baseball or in the local leagues in their backyard. One such organization, Baseball Town U.S.A., had no problem granting the "Greater Youngstown area" a charter in its Association of Honor.

Many of the old-time players, who played on the legendary baseball fields of Youngstown, Ohio, when steel ruled the world, when the field was shrouded by the charcoal black smoke pumped up into the sky by titanic smoke stacks, were indeed, legends in their own time. With some, those who played in the 1940's, 1950s's and early 1960's, their day of honor would have to wait for three or four decades, but it would come. In June of 1994, it finally came for then 65-year-old William "Billy" Olive.

The banquet held was a local affair, to honor the old-time inductees, but was attended by many major league players, coaches and scouts. Baseball, whether on a professional or semi-professional level, is a closely knit club of men with talent only given to one percent or less of the people placed on this planet. On the day of this affair, Billy Olive would be inducted and added to its Hall of Fame membership.

When Bill received his plaque, the inscription noted that he was "well known in baseball circles in both Pennsylvania and Ohio," that he took his post-war time baseball teams to championships, and that he was one of the youngest players to pitch 3 no-hit ball games in the incredible leagues playing in Northeastern, Ohio, and Western Pa.

Billy took pride in his lifetime batting average of .300 and his service in the Korean war, along with his ability to pitch like a major league player.

Once, a baseball aficionado connected dots of the players inducted with Bill, and had no trouble linking him within three or four degrees of some of the game's great heroes of all time. Bill had the right stuff, but at the wrong time. When he returned from the service, a scout from the Majors came to Perkins Park in nearby Warren, Ohio, the home of Hall of Famer Paul Warfield and many other great athletes, to give the young 22 year-old pitcher " another look". Bill by then had injured his arm while playing in a cold spring game. He never could recover that magic left-handed curveball that attracted all that attention only a few years ago. But when he was healthy, he was really something to remember, and on that night in June of 1994, they did just that.

Billy Olive was, for some unknown reason, never one for bragging about his brush with greatness. He didn't mind telling you about this game or that championship, but it was always about the team and the league and other players, not just himself. The dust from these plaques and awards from that date accumulated next to his steel desk. The one Hall of Fame induction article appearing in the local paper was handed to me by the now 90-year-old star pitcher from Lowellville, Ohio. He felt it important enough to keep it for all these years, a sort of history that said yes, fifty years ago, I was there, I had my time, and I was good enough to make the grade. He was satisfied with that, and nothing more.

Chapter XXIII

THE DEGENERATE GAMBLER, BUT IN A GOOD WAY

T he first time Bill heard the word "Comp," he was already in that favored "client" clique'. The gambling establishments, the ones dominating the skylines of Atlantic City and Las Vegas, had very good accountants. Whether the Pink Flamingo, The Sands, Caesar's Palace, The Bellagio, The Venetian or any of the giants, they kept track of all things money related. If you were a "player", they knew about it. When you placed a bet on the crap tables, they knew when, which table your bet was placed upon and how much you wagered. When you sat at third base on the blackjack table, they had you covered. If you liked slots, as many elderly ladies from the Midwest and the Northeast did, they had your number. The pit bosses and progressively sophisticated "eye in the sky" software knew if you preferred the roulette table, one hundred-dollar slots, poker, poker, poker and, yes, even bingo.

They were not particularly interested in whether you were winning or losing, but how much and often you were laying cards down and donating to their establishments. If you were a "player", and came with a pocketful of money, and left with a little, and came back again, you were their preferred customer; And they treated you like one.

Billy would travel to Las Vegas and Atlantic City, often with his son Bill Jr., hundreds of times over the years. He never paid for his transportation, he never paid for his four star hotel suite, all the amenities the hotels had to offer were available around the clock, "on the house" and he had his own personal room service crew.

Some of the world's most delicious food, made by chefs recruited from the four corners of the world, was conjured up and featured at the luxurious restaurants embedded into the hotel properties on the Vegas strip. It was simply the best. A five-hundred-dollar tab for a meal in Vegas, at that time, would be a discount price. But with Bill, the high roller, it didn't matter. He never paid a dime. Since Vegas and Atlantic City are quite a way from your home, depending on what part of the country you are in, flying to these gambling meccas, round-trip, five days or more, would result in you dropping a few grand, for starters. Billy "O" never paid attention. "We make money on gambling, not renting hotel rooms or serving fresh seafood. This was the business model of the gambling industry; And it worked. I could just hear the bean counters say, in the early days, at the business meetings of the owners and financiers of these awesome adult playgrounds, " return business is the key, treat them like kings and queens." Billy as it were, was royalty in their eyes.

Billy "O" was a player. They knew Billy not for his suit and jewel fencing operations, or safe cracking, but for the amount of money he laid down at their gambling establishments. Chips could not fit in the pockets of the stolen suits he wore.

Yet, young William's gambling proclivity was not limited to the neon lights of Vegas or the Boardwalk hotels in Atlantic city. To be fair to Bill, he confessed that he was indeed a "degenerate gambler." He would bet on the weather, how many deaths would be recorded in a year, (He could have worked as an executive for any life insurance company in the United States") on political races, horse races, greyhound races, football games, baseball games, basketball games, hockey games, college sports games and even enjoyed flipping the dice against the brick walls in the back alleys of in his hometown. He couldn't get enough, and that was the problem.

I don't know many non-gamblers who would spend a day following Brinks security trucks, until they could use a stolen key to open its contents, spending it all within a day or so at one of these gambling houses. Many of us would not know people, unless they were addicted to gambling, looking through the yellow pages, as he and his crew would ride through a strange town, picking out stores that would be targeted for a heist for the sole purpose of taking their ill gotten gains to the nearest gambling house. I personally don't know men who would crawl on their bellies on a carpeted floor, while a heist was in progress, just to take "that hard earned money" from that job, and put it on a color of a small almond sized pea that would spin round and round, on a wheel, just to place a wager on where it would land. The cost of that joy, in Billy's life, was hundreds of thousands of dollars, if not more. As a man of numbers, Billy "O" calculated his loss to be over one million dollars during his perfect season. This didn't include money he gave to his tag along partner, his son Bill Jr. Although his son would never, ever, ever be part of the crew, taking

Bill Jr. on gambling jaunts with him was the only way he could spend, at the time, quality time with his only son.

Billy "O" was either a lousy player, or had the worst luck, or a combination of the two. A forty year ride on that roller coaster left him stone cold broke. One friend suggested, sometime in the early 1970's, that Billy "should just mail these places a check every year," and save on the time it took to travel there. He would lose those sums anyway. Why bother making the trip? Bill would just laugh as he boarded the next plane with thousands in his pocket, all destined to be food to feed the monsters of the midways in those towns of ill repute that he loved so much. Everyone has their vices, but with Bill, it was a way of life.

Chapter XXIV

DOWN THE RABBIT HOLE

Somewhere along the way, when rumbling along the thin back alleys at a location near his latest heist, Billy "O", like Alice, would never see it coming. He would fall deep down into the rabbit hole, sliding into the chute and coming out in a land where everything was upside down; Billy was being launched into the middle of a psychedelic dream. "Billy "O" enters the candy colored casino, with marshmallows on the roof, kaleidoscope walls and moving floors. He makes way for the tables of chance, as the big eye in the sky follows him from above. He could hear the voice of Pinky, imitating Alice, warning him of danger from imaginary people and strange things. "Billy, they know you are coming, you shouldn't be there, the house always wins." Billy "O" heads for the lush green surreal coverings of the gambling tables. They appeared so large, and he, so small, that Billy could only surmise he was in the middle of some well maintained, but oddly shaped golf course. As he rumbles to make his play, two large dice, the size of marble monuments, with liquorice embedded into the dented holes of each, are rolling toward him. He can't get out of the way. He screams as the dice nearly roll over him. He was spared when a small squirrel pulled him down into his security hole. Billy pops up and turns to look for his favorite slot machines, the high roller ones, the one hundred dollar ones, the five hundred dollar ones.

In this real, imaginary land, the slots are floating around in space, untethered and free, as players in hot air balloons try to navigate toward them, dropping in silver money with the help of blue birds carrying the coins. The arms on these surrealistic flying machines need to be pulled. " Billy, get out of there, you are going to get hurt." " I like it Pinky, I know how to play and I love it." Billy leans over the carriage of the hot air balloon as he tries to pull the squishy slot levers down. He grabs onto the candy covered nob, and as he pulls with all his might, he loses balance and begins his fall out of the carriage, speeding perilously toward the ground. "I told you big brother, these places are not for you!" As he speeds to meet his doom, the gaming mansion flips, as the master thief falls up and into the ceiling made of sticky cotton candy. A blue bird flying by whispers in his ear. "Billy, you have to leave, now!" "Billy, the man at the door doesn't want you here, the one with the diamond shaped hat, the one walking on paper stilts." " Billy, you just lost a thousand dollars on this flying machine." "But I love it Pinky, watch me fly."

Billy pushes off the ceiling and swims toward an island near the coast of casino-land. There are formal dinner tables lined up on the peach colored sandy beach, as if at a banquet of some sort, attended to by pretty little penguins dressed in their formal tuxedos. They sit motionless as they await their guest who has just emerged from the purple colored water. He takes a seat at a three dimensional black jack table. "Pinky, I always lose at blackjack, but I can't stop." "I love it." Orange, crimson, deep black and ruby red cards are flying through the air like arrows, being dealt by a young girl with long, rubbery arms and snakes nesting in her medusa-like head. "Billy, duck! Those cards are as sharp as razors, they will slice you in half before you can play your first hand." "Duck Billy, he will kill you. Here they come!" The King of Hearts and the Ace of Spades were streaking toward him like stealth military drones, cutting off the heads of daring penguins who stood in their way. "Out of there get you, young man!" "Wait! Here comes the Jack of Diamonds and an Ace, I can't lose!" As the cards fly toward the ex- Military Policeman, out of a forest of teal colored rubber trees comes a horseman, minus his head, wielding an ax." The madman is galloping full speed toward Bill. "Watch your head Billy, he is the dangerous phantom!" Bill, rising up from his chair, stumbles backwards and takes cover. He is spared the swift swinging blows of the shiny ax, as he falls back, and to the left, into the sea. The horse upon which the ax wielding nightmare rides upon, stops at the beginning of the shoreline. He can't swim, yet. Billy hallucinates within his dream. He is back in the navy vessel that traversed the oceans towards South Korea. He feels safe there, thinking he is hiding safely under the candy colored sea, plotting a course that would take him back in time in a desperate attempt to reclaim his lost love, Sun-yee.

As Bill finally disembarks from the Navy frigate and onto the shores of MacArthur Park, he takes his first step onto the land he once knew. As his foot hits the bloody ground, Billy is spinning out of control, running round and round, caught up in a spinning circle. A granite ball of sorts is rolling fast and furious, toward him. William George Olive is losing wind as the wheel spins around faster and faster. He stumbles, glides and leeps over red, then black squares, caged in iron wire, keeping ahead of the black granite pea. He hears it thumping and pinging as the wheel begins to slow, its death rattle now unmistakable. "The pea is landing on Blood-Red 21", as he tries to jump off the table. "Always bet Black Billy," the voice over the microphone warns. Unable to keep pace and out of gas and glory, he is nearly crushed by the bouncing pea, as he falls off the table and opens his parachute from training camp, before hitting the hard tile and marble tacked to the ground of this strangest of places.

Billy "O", athlete, soldier, family man and master thief, is taken prisoner by four heavily armed guards. They are dressed in oversized North Korean uniforms. They begin torturing him. The guards unload thousands of dollars into his lap, and beg him to place bets on games that are rigged. He is assured he will win if he bets, and that he will keep all his winnings. He is there for an eternity, coming within an inch of winning at each throw of the die, or flip of the card. Yet this sugar coated promise of instant fame and millions of dollars is only, in the end, a perpetual illusion.

"Run Billy, run!" "I can't. My legs are strapped with iron and steel locks. My hands are cuffed behind my back." The ceiling of the three dimensional gambling parlor begins its push downward. After a short time, the moving floors grind upward, like a submarine surfacing. The marshmallow walls turn to stone, engraving permanent etchings into the wiley floor now closing in on young William Olive. "It's all a rich man's game Billy; You can't win!" "It was never about winning Pinky, it's the thrill little sister, the thrill of it all." "It makes me feel alive!" "This ain't baseball Billy, and these people are trouble." A fox, like the ones he used to trap back home in the hills of nearby Pennsylvania, trots up to Billy Olive as time is running out. "You let me go once before, after catching me in that spring trap up in the hills behind your father's home. I owe you. Listen to me." The fox was dressed like one of them, in a neatly tailored suit; A bowtie with a starched collared shirt, topped by a gentlemen's black hat, looking just like Abe Lincoln, completed the imaginary image. " You have one chance, go toward the light Billy, it's the only way." "I am ..I am trying, but I can't move my foot and the light is fading away from me!" Young William George Olive was lost in a world he loved, one that made him feel alive, but was destined to become the very means of his demise. He loved all things that would injure him. Although flat broke after making millions, his mind kept lying to him, aggressively arguing that in the end, it was all worth the price of admission; And it wasn't.

As total silence commanded the air, the voice of Grace Slick was heard in all its wondrous pitch and glory, louder than the horns of Jericho.

"And the white knight is talking backwards,

And the Red Queen is "off with his head", Remember

What the dormouse said,

Feed your head…...Feed your head……Feed your head……"

Get out of there Billy!

Chapter XXV

"We Play In A Band"

The crew always made it a point to fly to Atlantic City after a successful heist. This time was no exception. As the five well-dressed dapper men headed to their now familiar seats, one of the stewardesses, who made it a point never to ask personal questions, finally gave in. "You know, you fellas fly this same flight and sit in the same seats at least twice a month. Can I ask you what you do for a living?" Billy "O" again, didn't miss a beat. "Sure doll. We play in a band." The stewardess seemed confused. "Oh yeah, what's the name of your band?" Billy, half speaking half laughing, proudly replied, "Billy 'O' And The Rooftoppers. We have many big hits. You must have heard of us." The crew broke out in laughter, as they smiled at the TWA blonde. Unbeknownst to anyone on the flight, the crew had just robbed a safe, breaking in through a hole in a large retail store, and stealing a truckload of women's clothes and high end jewelry. The only way the police knew it was the crew from Lowellville was by their unmistakable "in your face" trademark. They had stolen the clothes off the store window mannequins, again. That became the band's calling card as they continued their run in the midwest and beyond. It was 1971, and the hits just kept on coming.

Chapter XXVI

Finding Billy O.

nd so I am reading my notes, and admittingly chuckling at times, then bursting out with laughter at these most excellent capers. My handwriting should be a tool for the C.I.A, for only I could decipher it. I am running my eyes over my scratchy words, some printed, others script, telling the tale of when a well-known businessman, with the best store in a town in upper Northwestern Pennsylvania, near the border of New York State; As he walked into his establishment, the shelves, the hangers, the inventory, the light bulbs and everything made of atoms, were missing from the store. To him, it looked like a hollowed-out garage. He surmised that he must have entered the wrong store. He rushes out the front door, walks to the next door down, thinking maybe he had too much to drink the night before. No dice. Billy and his crew, four streets away with field binoculars, were laughing their ass off, as the entire contents of the medium size retail operation were being wheeled away in an unidentified semi tractor-trailer truck. Too much!

I read on.

Billy "O", most notes allege, was a savant, a master with numbers. He liked to count things. Two hundred and sixty-six thousand suits. Two-hundred sixty-six thousand suits..I call bullshit, Billy "O"! He looks at me, "No, do the math, four decades, two or three times each weekend, I can even tell you the stores and cities." "Bullshit Billy 'O'." "Ellwood City mall, mid 60's, last store on the right, suits. The men's store in Mt. Vernon, suits- one hundred stuffed in the back seat and one hundred suits in the trunk. Two cars. Four hundred suits. It was too easy. I went back the next day, Sunday." "No one saw you? Come on?" "It was a small town. In and out. And we had two big cars. Just like that." "The warehouse in Kentucky, if my crew didn't forget to pay the night watchman, we could have stolen one thousand suits every weekend. But we did get a ton." My unreadable, illegible note taking, continued. Southwoods City, Maryland, suits. Tractor trailer, full of suits; make sure the blinkers and headlights are working, tires just right, no chance of getting pulled over...suits.....a truck container. That's a lot of suits. Forty years of suits, every weekend, do the math pal. I ain't bragging, it was just something we did in those days."

I flip through my yellow pad. (Never write with a black flair pen.) I trace over some letters, it's worse. I squint. Bill states that "if you borrowed a semi- tractor trailer of cartons of cigarettes, twice a week, you would make a half a million dollars today." "One time, when pall malls and lucky strikes were the hard nose cigarettes, we hit a warehouse in Northern Pa. The fella we paid knew when the truck was coming in. So I am walking out..(illegible) it took two hours, and it was a ton of cigarettes and the company was up in arms and the police were all over this the next day and I am thinking, those two ladies, they saw us, this could be the one that breaks the streak." "We always dress nice and be nice. Always. Later I heard and read that two ladies told these cops that they saw two people fitting our description

(Benny and me) going in and out of that warehouse for most of the day. They told the police "Yes, they were very nice gentlemen." "They spent all afternoon, it seemed, taking cigarettes from a large truck and stacking each case neatly in that store across the street." Mother of Mary. How could they not know Billy? "We were nice to them, always be nice."

And so now I am a cheerleader of sorts. "Go on Billy "O", tell me some more. Just mix some truth with those lies, then I could work with it."

"On 'safe' jobs, for some reason, the grocery stores in the area always kept $20-25 thousand dollars cash in their safes. No more, no less. I could name the stores and where they were located." "Remember, at that time, $25,000 was worth almost $90,000 in today's money." "Where did it all go?" "Did you ever gamble?" "300 times, Atlantic City, 150 times, Las Vegas, local gambling, around the clock, in between jobs. I once had a straight flush and everyone folded on the first round. There was only eight bucks in the pot. I am the only guy in the country that ever won eight bucks with a straight flush!"

Look up "Bobby Brooks." ("Note to self- was sketched on the left side of the margins on page 22.)"Women's clothes, easy to wear, big thing.... late 1950's and 1960's. "We boosted the best women's ready to wear outfits in four to five states, over and over. Housewife dresses. Evening dresses. Ladies tops. Twelve times in two states, semi-tractor trailers. We could have opened our own "Bobby Brooks" retail store. But it was easier to fence and collect." There was a place in Cleveland. We would drive by this big house in the suburbs, and there would be a large window in the basement. It was never locked. We must have been there ten times a month. It was a hell of a fencing operation. We always got paid. We would back up the truck, and start to carefully slide the clothing down the back ramp of the trunk, and right into the shoot and down into the cellar. We never once, out of all those times, saw anybody. We just put thousands of the best women's garments in the United States down that hatch, and would be paid by someone, every time. Never stiffed. To this day, I would not know who in the hell lived in that house. But I do know they had a warehouse full of dresses deposited in that cellar. Hope it was a big one."

I am looking at my yellow pad notes, again, something about a huge safe and the rest of my notes run on to another page- that I just spilled coffee on. "Bill, you had all this technology, why would you....?" "You're talking about the time they changed the direction on the pin that opened the safes? It was always lined up at twelve o'clock, once you punched through, now it was at eleven o'clock. I know these grocery safes have $25, 000.00, so I am not just leaving." " This happened at a store in Pittsburgh when I had a dump truck with a high lift, tagging along for this job. Now this safe had to be full, it was the new larger, heavier, safer-safes. I knew it was eleven o'clock at the pin. We wouldn't have time to use blow torches on the metal that was on this one. We knocked a hole in the back of the store's cement wall, hit the reverse gear, put the hoist onto the safe, and lifted it up and dumped it in the back of the truck. The other thing you had to do was make sure the dump truck had large wooden running boards, very, very high, but not too high, to make sure no one saw the safe sticking above the boards as you were driving it to the location where you could use the plasma torch to peel it open." " Sure enough, one time a local black and white pulled next to us. They looked over and saw me and Benny. I think I waived at one of them. We were just two guys trying to make a buck. They waved back. The high backboards worked. We went to Vegas twice that month."

My chicken scratch continued onto the back of the next page. "One time, we took a brand-new toilet seat, from a construction site, and used it as an outhouse at a camping ground when we went up into the hills of New York to a cabin. We stayed there for a while, did some tracking and hunting and had a relaxing time. That was the best heist ever." "I took it with us when we left after burning the place down for the insurance money. I owed a favor to a friend."

OK, Bill..OK. I buy that one. Let's move on.

Chapter XXVII

THE BEST TOYS

et's face it, there came a time when the Feds and their technology were making it a more fair game of cops and robbers. The farm boys wearing suits in Oldsmobiles, coming to Ohio like a one hundred car train, steaming through the Ohio turnpike, one after another, without paying the toll. To be fair, that was their job. One didn't expect FBI agents to be organizing property theft rings and creating fencing operations for stolen goods. Their job was to find those people that did these things and put them in jail. By the same token, Billy "O" didn't wear a badge, was not a military policeman any longer, and was not in charge of locking up all the safecrackers in the Midwest and east coast. Yet like baseball players on opposite teams, they did, ironically, use many of the same tools in applying their trade.

The Feds improved their game quite a bit, other than the one incident where Billy switched their tracking device from his car to one vehicle carrying two law-abiding citizens enjoying a day on the road. But their tracking techniques were improving. On the other hand, safes, with all their improvements, including thicker metal and iron walls, were still no match for Billy "O". "Judge, we need this warrant. It's one of the outfits on the top fifty; The safecrackers. We have received information from an informant where there are criminal tools, very sophisticated, being stored." Before the agent could finish, the local judge gave the joint task force, (Local cops working with the F.B.I.,) just what they wanted- a search warrant to rip apart the William Olive property in Lowellville, Ohio.

Billy had a camper, and like many people, he kept it in the back of his driveway. But unlike other people, I don't think Billy "O" used the camper for family picnics at parks and other national places of interest. In fact, this is the famous camper, or one just like it, where Billy would park in some city in upper Michigan, as he watched, from the back of the camper's vinyl pull up scratchy black shade, the comings and goings of the police and customers of a women's fine jewelry store.

The search warrant permitted the Joint Task Force to raid Billy's premises, based upon probable cause that these "criminal tools" were on the premises. The true intent of the warrant, I would wager, was that the tipster fibbed that a sixteen wheel tractor trailer rig, full of something, was heading Billy's way, maybe another quick "stuff it all in the house" routine, where the agents could catch one of the "most wanted" in the act. (And this, he was.) The agents pulled five or six cars in front of Bill's home, pistols out, papers waving, young screeching voices of farm kids announcing who they were and why they were there, creating drama that not even the neighbors themselves, by this time, could ignore. Yet, much to the agents' chagrin, there was no tractor-trailer rig container storing hundreds of stolen items shipped across state lines. What they did find instead, were highly sophisticated tools for use in safe cracking operations.

Billy stood on his front lawn, watering his flowers. He chatted with some of the agents, thankful, no doubt, that his house was not presently used as an inventory warehouse for the "hottest" fashions of the day. But his concern grew proportionately as the agents stumbled around, back toward the end of his driveway and into his backyard where his camper was stored. The "rat" that gave the information to the law enforcers, Billy thought, told him about the camper.

One of the new agents, like a kid at Christmas time, expecting a gift that he specifically asked Santa for, looked under the camper in a storage area. He clicked it open. "Holy shit". The crew of agents rumbled toward the camper, as the various "tools" were pulled out from under its spidery bottom undercarriage. The wares were now in full view, an image similar to a vendor showing his goods at the county flea market. There were torches, pulleys, big black safe peeling bars, oxygen tanks, hammers, crowbars and something else. Something so interesting that the senior Fed himself, attached to the operation, approached Bill and inquired about it- a particular torch and oxygen tank in plain view. "Hey, we have never seen a blow torch and mirror like this one. This must cut steel like a knife through hot……". Bill interrupted. "It's pretty good, they say." " "Those black bear crow bars, we can't find one in any hardware store in three states. How many of these do you have?" " I don't know what you mean." " You were, and I am just guessing, going to use them, so the other competitors wouldn't, and knowing you Mr. Olive, you probably would sell them back to those same rival crews once you got what you came for." The junior agent, new on the job, chimed in. "Hey, that is a plasma torch, hot as hell. Is this the one I read about in the newspaper article?" "They're not mine." As the agents tried to question Bill, he interrupted them, and in a polite but sarcastic manner, quipped, "You like them so much, take them, they're yours now."

"Why don't you talk to us Bill?" "You know, without your stool pigeons, you guys couldn't make half your cases. "No, Mr. Olive. We would only make five percent of them."

Chapter XXVIII

MUSICAL CHAIRS

"We stole vending machines, poker machines, anything that ate quarters and dimes and nickels, and emptied them, but the best part, we eventually made our way back to those same places and sold their own machines back to the establishments we took them from. Now that is what Recycling is all about."

The great thing about vending machines is that they can make a joint a bunch of money. If you put a dollar in change in a vending machine, for a soda or candy bar, you can believe the house made fifty cents on that dollar. Since the beginning of time until now, no other invention could do the things a vending machine could do. Every restaurant, bar and social club in the entire Ohio, Western Pa. and W.V. areas had vending machines. There were hundreds, if not a thousand or two of them. Candy and Soda pop were not the only items that this "retail in a box" could dispense. There was the "claw" that grabbed the toys on the bottom of the glass box, the worthless trinkets, fake jewelry, candy, you name it. It was pure profit, they cost next to nothing to buy or steal. After a short time, the inventive minds of the local mafia figures had another use for these portable money makers. Poker.

One machine manufacturing company discovered that it could produce vending machines that would allow you to play games of chance or skill. From pinball, to poker, and other fun games, the coins would stream in, resulting in large profits for that particular establishment. Month after month, the owners of the machines would lease them to these bars and restaurants. They made money on the lease and a share of the profits. They sent their "people" around to empty the coins from the machine and split the dough. When you make your customers and partners happy, everything is fine. Soon, the vending people, not the type you would find in the front row at church, would envision a better profit margin program for the machine.

Poker games are fun to play. Poker games that pay off, if you beat the machine, are more fun. The only problem is that in those states during these times, this was a crime. It was and is called gambling. Unless the State of Ohio gives you a license to gamble, it's illegal. But when in Rome, Billy "O" did as the Romans would do. Billy and his crew " got into the vending business." He had machines that paid off money, but more often made money from degenerate gamblers who couldn't afford the bus fare to Atlantic City. The machines were golden, and the mafia did not like competition. But that didn't stop Billy Olive. But for some reason, the local mafia family representatives would rather partner with him, than fight him. They recognized efficiency when they saw it.

Hundreds of machines, thousands of dollars, each month. It was like paying on a mortgage. The machine was the bank and Billy was the bank clerk, taking in the deposits and splitting them with the shareholders. Yet with the laws of supply and demand at work, there were simply not enough machines to go around to all of the Inns, bars, and restaurants that needed them, that depended on them, for the extra profit to meet their overhead expenses. Soon, machines began to disappear. It was like a bidding war. If Billy knew he could get another location to pay more, that machine would be "transferred", without the bar keepers consent, to another location. It would remain there for a while. Soon, bar and restaurant owners begged Bill Olive's crew "to find me a damned vending machine. I need it to make the rent." They would make "new" arrangements if Bill could find them one, arrangements that put more money into the pockets of the crew.

Like the game of "musical chairs" played in grade school, when the music stopped, there was always the bidding war, the "removal, the recycling and relocating of the machine to another place." In the end, someone would always come up empty. After a time, Bill would be very careful, as many of the establishment owners who bought these "new machines", were close to learning that they were actually buying or leasing back their old machines, but at a much higher cost.

This business model would be cutting edge for Wall street, but for now, it remained a viable business plan for the crew operating in the streets of Mahoning County.

Chapter XXIX

THE BILL, FOR BILLY O.

Some of my laughter and interest in Billy's tales became a guilty pleasure.There are many good people who work their arse off, getting up at 6:00 a.m. and working five days a week. It wasn't fair to them to have to spend their hard money on prices of goods that may have been increased due to the boost in insurance premiums. In fact, after a time, it seemed like it was all total bullshit. Bill, did you ever think what you were doing was wrong. "Nah, I mean, we had our rules. We never robbed a bank, we never were like the thugs in the mafia, and I am ashamed of them as fellow countrymen, - never liked what they did, all the violence. Most importantly, "my one rule which would never be broken; we never entered anyone's home. That was another infamnia. (The unthinkable)."

Billy repeated his mantra of excuses. "So, the places we knocked off all had insurance, or they should have. The owner would make a claim to his insurance company, and most of the time, made it real high-inflated." " He made a few extra bucks off of the insurance company. The insurance people raised rates, and they would have,

131

anyway. This was just a way of life for a while." I wasn't buying it, but after reflecting for a minute, I had second thoughts. Maybe the old man, just maybe, had a point. This insurance business needed a guy like Billy "O", they wanted a guy like Billy "O" and they couldn't be in business without a guy like Billy "O". After all, it doesn't rain or flood every day. Fires happen. But in between, (and they would never admit it when gouging the public with increased premiums) they did require a "partner" like Billy "O". They didn't have the balls or nerves of steel that he had, or the expertise, and probably couldn't hit a baseball or throw a no hitter, but they had no problem jacking up those rates for theft coverage.

After much reflection, and a half hour break from trying to interpret my interview notes, some crazy over the top thoughts ran zig zag around the room, in and out of my head. "Who am I, who are we to judge Billy Olive?" I saw a Bible at the end of the table in my back office, "Judge not..and after all, he never killed or hurt anyone." Maybe Billy "O" was the price we paid for having a Bill Gates, or a Dr. Salk (Chief contributor to the polio vaccine) or better yet, maybe Billy "O" was the billing "invoice" or statement the universe had sent us, that was to be paid for every "Pinky" or "Pop Shraum" or "Dominic Olive", that enriched the lives of so many people. Maybe Billy "O" was the interest we paid on this debt of gratitude, for all we have and all we have enjoyed in life and all that is left to do. I thought further.

What if Bill had led his life backwards? What if we looked at his accounts and deeds in reverse? Surely, we would not hold anger toward an infant for removing a toy from a neighbor's shelf that didn't belong to it. And certainly, we would all say, "What a great man he is becoming, a wonderful example for young men of his age. Look, he is a star baseball player, and Mel Ott himself wanted him to play professional baseball; And my God, he passed that up to serve in the Korean

War, as a military police officer." "He could have died of dysentery on the way over to Seoul or could have been killed breaking up a bar fight. He kept the order. He helped fight the Chinese Communist. And, in the end, he had to leave one of the two loves of his life, Sunyee, to come back home to help his father's roofing company. What a romantic tragedy." His father, Dominic Olive who, with Billy's help, worked around the clock putting a roof on a three floor home for one entire summer, shredded the substantial bill for their services when the owner of the house was killed in an accident at work, leaving a wife and five beautiful children without him. "Spin the wheel of time and space, twist it around and fold it in half, a circular life analyzed, not the long, drawn out chronological tale we use to judge people. Maybe this is how the universe keeps score." They didn't look at the final inning and tally to see who won or who lost, they looked at the great hits and defensive plays in between. They looked at Billy helping his mother through the death of Pops Shraum. The maker upstairs saw the pain of Bill when his son passed. How about the people he helped with money problems later in life, or who came to him for advice after getting into street trouble? Billy delivered. He would later help a young person find her way in life, one who would become a lifelong friend. That and much more happened in the third or fourth inning, and heavenly fans saw those plays, although they may have purposely missed the late innings. One would surely have a different view of this man's life using those standards, rather than how we normally judge people. "Change the scoring rules, and we may have a different "most valuable player." "Play by the universe's score card and maybe, for once, we would be able to keep the command of not to judge another, lest we be judged."

Chapter XXX

A DIFFICULT CHILDHOOD; AND NOTES FROM THE TED O. INTERVIEW; RE: BILL JR.

B illy had been through some soul ripping experiences, all before the age of 29. Back when his father, the saint, oper- ated the family business with grandpa Shraum and young William, Bill's father was suffering from cancer of an advanced stage. In the late 1930's and early 1940's, the Colo-rectal cancer his father was tortured by was virtually incurable on its best day. Bill listened, with one ear open to the wind and the other buried in his pillow, to countless nights of moaning and pleading by his father to, it seemed, an unforgiving God. People in the village often heard him at night, swimming in his pain, unable to come up with a breath of relief. Meaningful medical treatment for colon cancer was at best, during this time, something characterized as non-existent and experimental. But no one could explain Dominic Olive's surrealistic extraordinary peaceful demeaner, as he went about a work detail that would fag out a young man half his age. No one was quite sure how Bill dealt with the daily opera of suffering his beloved father experienced. Yet one thing was for certain. Bill, deep down in his intuitive soul, where no one was permitted entrance, had subconsciously, despite his best efforts, felt the pain, sadness, loneliness and dred that this unwelcome visitor of doom brought to his father on a daily basis.

Those kinds of places hidden deep within the soul, are, out of necessity, a small place indeed. The lock that keeps them from infecting the whole of the body is one that could never be compromised. The death of his grandfather, which initially forced the leave of his senses, also needed a storage space before it destroyed the young man's entire sense of reality. In a murky sort of way, that too was placed under quarantine, and lasted for quite some time. Taking a one, two punch of heartache as this would be a combination that no man, with the exception of young Billy Olive, could survive. Some say the capacity for the human body and soul is vast, and is capable of assimilating much pain. But therapy sessions were for the Park Avenue crowd at that time, and ordinary Americans, like young Billy Olive, suffered in silence, not peeping a word about the herd of elephants in their room.

Yet, the passage of time would yield more suffering, more heart wrenching pain and suffering upon this young man. Upon the unbelievable sequestering of Sun-yee's last image from the center of his mind, some guessed that a change in several thousand miles of geography and a reunification with his wife tossed Billy, a life saver he barely caught. His resumption of life in America, although most would disagree, may have given him at least a chance of a new outlook on life. Those arguments all ended with the birth of his son.

Billy Jr. was Bill's only masculine child. His life in the shadow of emotional desolation finally had a chance of resurrection. Bill Olive Jr. was born a healthy, well-nourished boy. During his early years, when father Bill returned from his weekend jaunts, he played with young Bill like any doting father, all while hiding his pain, checking the locks on his secret places to ensure the beasts inside were never to see the light of day again. As the early fatherly years went on, Billy established a routine with his son. He would take him everywhere a young toddler should be taken, with each free minute he had. This would go on like clockwork until young Bill was of school age.

Ted Olson related the following: In the early 1960's, as young Bill went off to school, the local doctors conducted their usual examinations and administered the schedule of vaccinations given to all young school children at that time. The teachers, now better trained in observing children for any "unusual behavior", kept an eye on young Bill as time went on. When comparing young Bill Jr. with the other young boys and girls in his class, young Bill was considered just a bit slow in development relative to other children of his age and grade.

Bill Jr. and Ted were the same age. They rode the school bus together. Bill Jr. had various learning disabilities. He was always in special classes. When Bill did the 17 months in the Federal Penitentiary because of that "certain rat", Olive and Bill Jr. had to leave their home in Lowellville and go to nearby Campbell, Ohio, renting a house there. When Billy "O" got out of prison, (per my notes regarding the conversation with Ted. O.) he went back into the roof and gutter business with Bill Jr., now of an older age. Olive Olive, Billy's wife, remarried. Billy was always around the family; Olive's second husband died. Billy bought a house for his ex-wife and Bill Jr. They both lived there for years as Billy "O" lived separately in a house nearby them.

Ted related that young Billy worked with his dad, but never went with him out of town with the crew; Only local jobs in the roof and gutter repair industry. Bill Jr. went on to acquire and operate a spring water distribution business with his father. It was featured in the local press.

(My notes then jumped off the page.) Ted advised me that Billy Jr. had a drinking problem, and that he became a chronic alcoholic in the 1980's. It broke his heart as he watched, then helped young Bill, in vain, with this horrible addiction. Young Bill became a functional alcoholic as he aged into his 40's, with difficulty staying sober. His mother Olive took care of him. Olive and Big Bill told him to stop drinking; Ted watched young Bill drink himself nearer to death. After Olive, his mother, died, Ted confirmed that young Bill went "downhill." Many ambulance calls; Young Bill in horrible physical condition from drinking; Ambulance crew took him into emergency; Young Bill was just hours from death; Called big Bill; Had tears in his eyes and gave his son a strong speech about beating the drink; Billy made sure he ate food and young Bill was good for three or four months. My last note regarding Ted's observations was that young Bill could not recover, wasting away in body and mind. Death was once again at the doorstep of the Olive home.

Chapter XXXI

LOSING BILL JR.

O f all the coincidences in the world, Billy Olive married a young girl, whose first name was Olive. Billy "O"'s wife's legal name was now, yes, Olive Olive. Of course, no one, in particular, businesses or services that required one to fill out their name on the first line, would ever miss the oddity of, "Olive Olive." Most clerks would take up minutes to joke, or share the amusement with Mrs. Olive regarding her name. In fact, it was often estimated that in talking or explaining the origin of her name, Olive Olive, consumed over two and a half years of her lifetime.

Bill Olive and Olive Olive were married for thirty years. They had a good marriage, as Bill provided Olive with all the comforts of a home, nice clothes, (with the understanding that furs and diamonds could not be worn in public due to obvious reasons,) and a safe and friendly neighborhood in the scenic small town of Lowellville, Ohio. Olive Olive would come to terms with Billy's weekend activities, as they helped pay the bills, and much more, and she would thus not, in most cases, complain of his absence. She was a good companion for the former Major league baseball prospect and Korean war veteran, never arguing or doing anything that would jeopardize their family life.

Olive Olive bore Billy Olive two children, a boy and a girl. They had a normal, so to speak, family life, with all the ups and downs that came with life. In fact, being married to a master thief was no different than, say, having a plumber for a husband. One serviced toilets, the other stole millions of dollars from retail stores and jewelry outlets. Both men would be home for dinner and treat their wives with love and respect.

Growing up Olive, young Bill Jr. was a quiet boy. He largely kept to himself. Some of the educators diagnosed him as a special need's student, with a less than average I.Q. He had only a few close friends. His father, after a time, became his closest pal. Billy took young Bill Jr. to work with him, every day, when he was old enough to learn the family trade. Billy taught his son the gutter and roof repair business. This was the business his family had been in for almost eighty years at the time. This was the business Billy grew up with, working six days a week with Grandpa Shraum and his father Dominic. Now, another generation of Olive's would come on board and keep the beautiful little town by the Mahoning river, and its residential and housing stock, in wonderful condition. To this day, Lowellville, Ohio, with its tiny but well-kept houses, railroad tracks and green fields is nothing short of a "postcard" town.

Young Bill went everywhere with his father, except when Billy "O" went out of town. Billy "O" would never permit, allow, encourage or otherwise make his son part of his other life. That was an infamnia. (strictly forbidden). Billy "O" did not want his son in that life. Period. In point of fact, as time went on, and young Bill became a young man and married, Billy "O" helped establish young Bill in the bottled water business. These were the days when spring water, which was heavily monitored by the state government for safety, was a unique item, and one in demand. Young Bill took the reins of that company, often being featured in prominent newspaper articles and other publications, as one of the top spring water companies in that region of the country. The business was good for young Bill and young Bill was good for the business. Yet, something was not right, not by a long shot.

After a time of success in his business and his marriage, young Bill, now middle aged, began to drink heavily, and it was not the spring water. Bill began to lose weight, had numerous health problems and otherwise was well along the path of chronic alcoholism, a medical disease that is common in the United States, but not one that anyone likes to talk about; That is its most dangerous symptom, stigma.

After a bit more time, Bill Jr. became a functioning alcoholic, drinking around the clock just to maintain his sanity, although that was also fleeting and was something taken hostage by this disease. Olive Olive, before her death, was the caring mother she always was, now taking care of her son Bill on a daily basis. By now, it was 2014, and her baby boy Bill Jr. was like a walking skeleton. Many ambulance rides were had, taking her son to the hospital and back. His system, one doctor explained, was totally devoid of certain minerals that were necessary to maintain life. The lack of such would and could abruptly end young Bill's life.

Billy "O", by this time, as with many family members of alcoholics, was at a loss for what to do to return his loved one, young Bill, to a normal life. Billy "O" never one to become angry over much, a cool cucumber, whether at war, on a heist or pitching with the bases loaded, begged, pleaded, demanded and shouted at the top of his lungs for his son to stop destroying himself. This was the last of the many speeches Billy "O" would give his son. After more time, He and Olive would now hand feed their child, as when he was a toddler, as his condition continued to deteriorate.

But Billy "O" would not give up on his son. That was just an impossibility. Young Bill began to rally a bit, and was able to join his father on roof and gutter jobs once again. Some say it was a "blooming phase," often seen shortly before death. Yet all prayed that young Bill would have another chance at beating this monster.

At this time, Billy "O" had the daily routine established. During the week, Billy would drive to his son's nearby home, often calling when he was ready to drive over to gather him for a day's work. This went on for a bit, and a while longer. One Friday, Billy seemed to recall, or it may have been a Thursday, Billy called to tell his only son that he was coming over to pick him up. No one answered. At that time, Billy "O", with his sharpened intuition, absolutely knew tragedy had come to visit upon his young son. Billy pulled into his son's driveway. As he walked up to the back door, it was ajar, open, something that in all his lifetime, young Bill would never allow to occur. Billy walked into his son's home, slowly and then a bit quicker, and saw the body of his baby boy, now sixty-two, lying on the living room floor, the life in him expired. His struggle with alcoholism was over. Billy "O" now assumed the gut wrenching task of making all the necessary calls and arrangements for the burial of his son.

Billy "O", by 2015, was still an active, sharp and an intelligent man. Although eighty-five years old, he was still capable of using a hammer and a nail and doing repair jobs with his only son. Billy was always in control of his emotions. He had to be. Growing up and working with his father and grandfather, he did indeed witness his grandfather's tragic death at the railroad tracks in town. He experienced his father's long battle with cancer, the daily pain and suffering to which he had a front seat. Billy "O" left at least one unrequited love of his life, Sun-yee, back in the hell called Korea, as he was ordered home. He had nerves of steel, as a left-handed future Sandy Koufax would have. Nothing rattled Bill. Many at the time of his son's death commented that Billy "O" was a tough character, and he could take anything. Yet, when Bill saw his young son, his only son, lying in a coffin, death taking him away to some unreachable place, Billy "O", for the first time in his life, showed his poker hand. He cried like a baby. He cradled and touched his son's hand and was inconsolable. When his son was buried, a large part of Billy's heart was buried too. In a recent interview, Billy "O", when asked about his son's memory, lowered his head and said, " I think about him every day. Everyday."

Note to God: No parent should have to bury their child.

Chapter XXXII

THE CASE OF THE
MISSING LEFT SLEEVE

B illy had the longevity genes, for sure. His mother lived to 99 years; His sisters are in their 80's. If you survived the cancer during middle age, it was a sure bet you would come close to the three digits. At 90 years old, Bill still lives a meaningful life. He wakes in the morning, at his senior living complex, (where his sister Pinky lives down the hall), has breakfast and goes to a small building his family owns, somewhere in the middle of Lowellville. The building is stuffed with scrap metal and collectables. Bill loves scrapping. He can hold a piece of metal in his hand, calculate its weight, and determine its value in the scrap market of that day. He always had that kind of talent with numbers.

Yet, I can't help but think that each piece of scrap metal, that is placed in its own peculiar place inside this mysterious building, carries a single memory in Billy's long life. While he picks up each piece, a specific memory is brought up from the deep recesses of his mind. On any given Monday, as he picks up that first piece of scrap

143

metal, I am certain he remembers the time when the retail suit makers finally figured out that their huge warehouses, in a five-state area, were losing hundreds of suits from their monthly inventory. That first piece of scrap metal most assuredly conjures up the heist that did not appear quite as successful as it first appeared.

By the 1980's, Billy would routinely, every weekend, plan and rescue suits from large warehouses, let's say, in Kentucky, and sell them on the black market. On this occasion, Bill had the usual protocol in place. He came to town a day or two early, joined later by his crew. As night fell, Billy and the band entered the tin and rusted warehouse and pilfered three or four hundred suits. But, this occasion would turn out a bit differently. The crew, no doubt, indeed carried out four hundred suits that steamy night and loaded them into the truck's container. This time, as the driver began to exit the back of the building on a dirt road, one of the crew members who was preparing the suits for a safe transport, called for Bill. "Billy, come here for a minute. You won't believe this. What the hell happened?" Upon closer examination, the suit manufacturer, in anticipation of someone like Bill removing his stock, had manufactured these suits with one modification, the entire left sleeve of each of the four hundred suits was missing! Bill, poker-faced as ever, went through each one. He ordered the truck to be driven along the Mahoning River. He dumped all four hundred suits into its muddy waters. Billy "O" could not help but have a great laugh with his crew. He always admired smart people, even if as here, he was now a victim himself. Karma is a ....!

Chapter *XXXIII*

THE "SAFE" DOCTOR

After his second cup of coffee, Bill would walk to the back of his cement building, through the dusty air revealed by the morning sunbeam from the east window, and tinker with another odd, but heavy piece of scrap metal. His mind would often wonder, but always return to the subject of safes. If there were a hall of fame for safe crackers, Bill would be inducted in his first year of eligibility. Billy "O" could lecture on the old "T" safe, how the guts fell out when you turned the pin, as well as opening the newer models, which had contact wires to alert security companies that someone was tampering with that particular safe. As technology evolved, Billy "O" himself decided, in an abundance of caution, that he needed to go back to "safe cracking school, and that he needed to find the perfect teacher."

A certain nationally known home and security company, identified by its letters, was raking in the dough, and dominating the home and commercial property security market. This company simply had the best new technology, and had trained certain people on its payroll to maintain and improve this cutting edge technology, no matter what the cost. Yet, as with any company, the workforce changed from time to time. Some employees leave and transfer their skills to another profession, others are injured on the job, and, yes, finally, many people that reach a certain age, while still sharp as a tack in the quality of their thinking and training, retire. Sometimes they receive a letter from the company thanking them for their service. In older times, it was the gold watch or a bonus check. However, with this certain expert technician that worked for the alphabet soup title company, he never was thanked or really adequately compensated for the work he did and improvements he made for this hugely successful corporation. When this top expert in the new "high-tech electronic defense of safes" retired from his former company, he was not one who was content to stay home and water the lawn or go on long walks with his dogs. No, this man was looking for employment, and, as happenstance would have it, Bill was in the market, looking to recruit an expert to train his crew in the techniques created by the very company who developed them. The new hire was now on board.

Within a month or so, the gentleman who came out of his brief retirement, was paid a respectable amount of money for the excellent job he did in training Billy "O"'s crew in the latest maneuvers which could, and did, defeat these high-tech safety systems. I often wonder if Bill chose to pursue an upper management career in another field, what new, bold and creative innovations he would or could do. For now, though, after attending classes with the new teacher on payroll, his own crew could and did crack any safe on the open market. And their roll, despite these new technologies, continued.

Chapter XXXIV

THE NIGHT BEFORE
CHRISTMAS

I t was Christmas come early for the lads from Lowellville. Shortly after they graduated from Billy "O"'s high-tech safe cracking school, under the tutelage of one of the best minds of the day on that particular subject, the boys were out on job after job. They were consumed with the success they were having, and, one of them was so very much caught up in the hoopla, that he had forgotten to buy his wife a Christmas present. For that crime, there is no forgiveness!

As 90-year-old Billy Olive picked up his last piece of scrap for the day, and while navigating his way out of the dark, cluttered storage facility, he began to make way for the scrap yard and his daily pay. While on this mission, he passed the house of his old friend, now deceased, whom he had saved from a Christmas day disaster. Billy, when glancing at the now abandoned house, instantly recalled that particular Christmas Eve, and how they rescued their good fella from a huge, huge problem.

It was near midnight and that certain Christmas Eve and extremely cold. In fact, the weather records documented that it was one of the coldest days of the decade. Most people, law enforcement included, were at home with their families on this Christmas Eve, with their children making ready for Christmas day and the presents that usually came along with it. Billy's crew would be a little late coming home that Eve, completing a job in temperatures of -10 below zero F.

It's a Cardinal sin to forget your wife's birthday, and even worse to fog up on your anniversary date, but Christmas, that's another level. No matter what, never, ever, ever forget to get your wife a Christmas present; And Benny did. Now, this kind of offense, if convicted, would carry a life term, not in jail, but of an annual " reminder" of your mortal blunder and the retelling of your act of omission, that would occur at least once a year, each December 25th, for the rest of your life. Some men would rather face ten flat years in the pen, then suffer the penalty of being whipped by "the one who is to be obeyed." And so it goes that one of Bill's crew had indeed been remiss, having no Christmas present for his beloved wife for presentation on that next day. It was late on that Christmas Eve night, all the stores were closed and their clerks and credit card machines were all retired for the night. It is, without doubt, the one time in a long year where everything is closed, as men of good cheer are with their families, passing out early Christmas presents and guessing what kind of sweater grandma would give them that year. To make matters worse, Benny made the colossal mistake of calling his better half on a pay phone to inquire as to how the holiday plans were coming along. Now, without a Christmas present for the Mrs., the last thing you want to be doing is calling your better half and telling her you would be home soon. "Oh Benny, I can't wait for you to see what I, I mean Santa, brought you this year. I hunted in every store in town, and even went to western Pa. and up to Cleveland to find this present for you. You have been asking Santa to bring this for ten years! The kids know all about it. They can't wait to see the look on your face, and that goes double for me. Never mind the cost, I can always start a new savings account, and the kids didn't mind chipping in with all of their allowance money; And we can always get a new family dog. We love you that much!"

While the operator indicated that Benny had to deposit two more quarters to continue the call, Benny, with a pocket full of them, told his wife, "Honey, I have to go, I don't have any change, I will be home before you know it." Click. Now the pay phone Benny used was near a gas station. Calmly, and without much fanfare, Benny looked for a bridge, or high platform of some sort, from where he could jump. Try as he may, none where to be found. He considered walking across the roadway, and into the path of an oncoming speeding car. Maybe they would mistake him for a deer, but be late on the breaks, sending Benny to heaven and his wife to the insurance agent the next day to collect on his life insurance policy. After burial expenses, he calculated that there would be enough left to reimburse his family for the cost of the much sought after Christmas present, whatever it might have been. But on that Christmas eve, not a soul was to be found on the road, as most normal people were home with their loving wife and family. Benny panicked.

It was times like these that "tried men's souls." Benny sheepishly walked over to Billy's car, as he was leaving for his own home. "Bill, I need a favor." Now some friendships are based on money, and loyalty comes with a price. But that night, Billy and the crew came through for their friend. Benny would never forget being pulled out of the fire that night by his friend Billy "O". Local history would go on to record that Benny and his wife would remain married for fifty years.

"It wasn't a marriage counselor we had to thank, it was the best heist man in the country." His wife would indeed receive a Christmas present the next morning, in fact, it was quite a magnificent present, "shining" as bright as the Christmas star itself. "God bless us, everyone", he thought, as the 1935 version of Scrooge ended its broadcast from a brand-new, state of the art high definition zenith television he had "picked up" only a few hours ago. His wife lived to watch those old Christmas movies, and that Christmas was a special one, her husband now nominated for sainthood upon the heels of surprising her with the brand new television set. Christmas is and was a season of miracles, and Benny now had just the right story to prove it.

Chapter XXXV

BILLY'S RULES

ruck heists, or taking, without the permission of the driver
or owner, control of a semi-tractor trailer load of goods, was
always a staple on the weekend menu of Billy's crew. Trucks
in that day had surpassed trains as the best means of transportation of goods in the economic boom of post-world war II America.
Trucks transported everything. They were made larger and larger,
their containers, or trailers, were made higher and wider, and local
and state laws permitted them to travel the highways with an unlim-
ited amount of tires and pure tonnage. On many occasions, politicians earmarked money to enlarge the size of the bridges and roads
crossing America's highways, to accommodate the teamster's union
and all of its members, as they all were, in the end, voters. After all,
without trucks bringing the everyday goods to the stores and shops
of America, the entire economy, based upon consumption of "things",
could not function.

When Billy Olive and his band were not out on a caper involving
jewel heists, and other such nonsense, hijacking or boosting trucks

was a skill they also had perfected. Yet, hijacking a truck and turning that venture into money, cash money, involved much more than met the eye. One must remember that any "run of the mill" thug could grab a truck and hit the highway, police in pursuit, with it all ending badly in terms of jail sentences and oranges and tomatoes squashed all over the payment of city streets. Billy was a pro. If you were going to hijack a truck, Billy had one main rule; It better be worth it.

If he had written a manual on how to engage oneself in the truck heisting profession, one could assume it would go something like this: Rule no. 1. If you are going to "borrow a truck", you needed to first find out what was inside the vehicle. This rule made a lot of sense to me. Suppose my crew and I hijack a truck, took it to a location known to only a few, and opened it-finding it contained a non-valuable commodity, like leftover fabric torn into unusable pieces or frost damaged produce, (for the sake of argument); The risk and investment of time and money would have all been in vain. Billy followed the first rule by making sure he established the proper business relationships with the teamsters who dispatched trucks from various areas in the Midwest to the Youngstown, Ohio, area. A well informed informant, one could say, would be able to tell the crew what trucks were coming into the area, what were they carrying in their super large containers, how many drivers or security people were on the delivery, what was the exact route the truck would be taking, what time was it scheduled to leave, how many other stops would it make, where was its final destination and how many trucks, if more than one, were in the convoy.

A good truck heist begins with knowing all of these particulars. Rule no. 2 would cover a detailed examination, using other sources along the turnpikes, of where the trucks would stop for a break, i.e. which truck stops along the route would be used for refueling or resting, and who was the chief of police in those areas and what was the color, license plates and description of the drivers. Rule no. 3 involved whether there was any other competition on this job, specifically, were other people in Billy "O" 's business targeting a particular load of goods? If so, Billy would need to know. There were plenty of trucks to go around for everyone during those days. Sub silencio communication between thieves is a matter that needs to be handled with care and trust. If handled correctly, everybody wins. Rule no. 4 of these basic rules involved how old the truck was- the last thing the crew wanted was an older truck that could not travel at top speed or may be susceptible to breaking down on the highway. Finally, Rule no. 5 covered the resale value of the truck. A newer truck would be able to be "resold" after various identification markers were changed or eliminated, and when its contents were safely inventoried and transferred to the proper fencing operatives. Only then could the truck be sold.

After these preliminary matters were resolved, Bill and his crew would arrive in advance at the appointed rest stop. They were well versed in hot wiring trucks in case the driver took the keys inside of the truck stop with him as opposed to leaving them under the passenger seat floor mat. Picking the lock to get into the truck was not a concern. Once the truck was driven away, Bill would time how long it would take to get to the drop off point. There, the truck's contents would be stored in a reliable place, and the new owners of the merchandise and possibly the truck, only if they were interested, would be readied for resale. If the truck was, for any reason damaged during the operation, it would be dumped in a park or into a lake or mining quarry in Pennsylvania or Lowellville.

Chapter XXXVI

THE FEDS AND THE
TOLL BOOTH

The crew from Lowellville always had a good run each month. The heists pulled by Billy Olive and his bunch had nothing to do with luck. But a new political development, one affecting law enforcement, was about to go down. J. Edgar Hoover, the long time Director of the F.B.I. announced the country was launching a war on organized crime. Before the public exposure of the infamous meeting of the five families in upper state New York in 1955, Director Hoover and other top F.B.I. officials down played the existence of what they knew was an extremely large criminal organization with tentacles reaching out across the entire United States. Las Vegas, as most people would come to know, was financed and built by the mob using Teamster Pension Fund monies, approved and hand delivered by Jimmy Hoffa himself. Bad publicity was something J. Edgar did not like, ever. Soon, the call went out to recruit a new, young brand of federal agents to fight organized crime. The main areas targeted outside of New York City included Chicago, Pittsburgh Pa., through to Cleveland, Ohio,; With a target painted on the back of the CIty of Youngstown. Youngstown was dead center in the middle of it all, as the cash earned by steelworkers financed the country-wide effort of the La Cosa Nostra. Many mobsters had problems with this new law enforcement effort, but the maverick Billy "O", for better or worse, had an idea to deal with this new scrutiny.

The world headquarters for the recruitment, training and swearing in of F.B.I. Agents was located at the now famous Quantico, Virginia, F.B.I. operations base. Agents were screened, trained, and prepared at Quantico before being sent to Northeastern and Midwestern cities to fulfill the Hoover directive of crushing the so-called Mafia, whose existence he once denied. (Rumor had it that the "La Cosa Nostra" was in business with Hoover, while also possessing compromising photographs of him in various dresses and situations with other people.) Thus, there existed for many years, a de-facto "blackmail" scenario of sorts. (Either Hoover backs off, or the photos are released.) For one unknown reason or another, public pressure, in particular from the Kefauver Commission, (and the work of future Attorney General Robert Kennedy) changed this dynamic. War on the mob and their associates was officially declared. The Mafia figures, including those in Youngstown, Ohio, were now the target of this new federal effort.

In the 1950's, President Eisenhower ordered the construction of a U.S. national highway system. The fear of nuclear war and the inability of people living in major U.S. cities to seek shelter in the countryside, accounted for this massive federal program that picked up steam in the 1960's and 1970's. As it were, this new and improving highway system and its "paid" turnpike routes produced millions of dollars for the states, as well as thousands of "toll booth jobs" that boosted the American economy. This vast improvement of our national highway system would also assist the F.B.I. in dispatching their agents in a more efficient and timely manner to these suspected centers of organized crime. This was bad news for Mahoning County and nearby areas which hosted major organized criminal activity.

Back in the day, and currently, the best route for tourists travelling from Northeast, Ohio to Washington D.C. involved using these paid turnpike routes running through West Virginia, Pennsylvania and eventually Ohio. When you pay to drive on these beautifully maintained roads, someone has to be at the various locations to collect the money through the window of the traveler's car. Toll booth workers made a decent living, and eventually formed a fairly powerful union. They had their modest shacks and familiar toll booth mega centers, or sole collection stations, near the exits of various major cities. Whether travelling to the Capital, or being dispatched to Youngstown, Ohio, and on to Cleveland, you would have to pay the toll. No exceptions.

Most toll booth workers are on autopilot, and barely notice any characteristics of the hundreds or thousands of drivers or occupants who pass through their gates during an average day. That was just a fact of life. They collected the money and opened the gate. That was their job. Every two weeks, most if not all of them received their check for a job well done. However, the toll booth workers who happened to be stationed along exits that were near the border of Pennsylvania and Ohio, and at exits to towns such as Pittsburgh, Youngstown and Cleveland, received a bonus check, or cash payment, on a weekly basis, from "other sources." Soon, these toll booth workers became valuable scouts for people like Billy "O".

In the 1950's through the 1970's, the local police departments and officers who patrolled the city streets of the Youngstown, Ohio, area did their jobs, keeping people safe, giving tickets to speeders, investigating traffic accidents and performing other rather routine daily duties. However, the steel boom in Youngstown made the city of steel, a cash cow. Each payday, hundreds of thousands of dollars were pumped into the local economy by the U.S. Steel producers, transferring rightful sums to workers who gave hard days of work in, many times, unsafe conditions. With the rise of the steel union, their wages went up. Many steel workers liked to gamble, many of them liked to buy suits at half price. Many of them liked women other than their wife. It was easy pickings for local gangsters. Yet the point of the matter was that organized crime, or as Billy "O" would say, "unorganized crime", was running rampant.

You would never see a police officer breaking up a poker game, unless the protection money was not paid to the designated police officer in a timely manner. You would never see Police detectives investigate stolen property rings, or other fencing operations. The fact of the matter is that when tips of this nature came in, the police officers, in all likelihood, grew up in the same neighborhoods as the very "suspects" they were asked to investigate. The law men were not about to put their lifelong friends from the neighborhood into harm's way. It became a more uncomfortable situation when the houses of prostitution, gambling and other vice operations were being operated or patronized by fellow police officers and, in some cases, police lieutenants and chiefs. This was life in places like Youngstown, Ohio, as well as across the Pennsylvania border, and down along the river to Steubenville and back. It was a free for all, and many of these organized operations never feared being pinched. As an ace up their sleeves, if they were pinched, and it was usually during election time for all the obvious reasons, "friendly" judges and carrier pigeon lawyers would make sure their "friends" did not serve one day in jail. If there was a more corrupt place in the world at the time, no one could locate it.

Chapter XXXVII

SURVEILLANCE
SCHOOL REDUX

H oover's young agents, keen on busting up organized crime and trained in the latest tactics, would be sworn in at very respectable and patriotic ceremonies at the "Q" before receiving their assignments. Once they did, (most of them were directed to these aforementioned areas in northeast Ohio,) they proceeded to drive to their destinations, all in the same make and color of unmarked cars, complete with special "red stenciled" designated license plates. The makers of certain Fords and Chevys were the standard, boring vehicles issued to these new agents. They all looked alike and so did the agents. Every agent, virtually all men at the time, wore the standard dark suit, black tie, no facial hair and top hat, with a trench coat if the weather dictated, as they proceeded up the turnpike from Quantico Virginia, stopping and paying the toll at each exit, and going on to the next toll both toward their destination. (The rumor, later confirmed, was that it was not enough that these agents were in the same types of cars, dressed the same, had the same kind of license plates and looked like farm boys from Virginia in Sunday suits. They had one other distinguishing characteristic. The new "G" boys foolishly abused the apparent authority they possessed; They were mooches, as they never paid the tolls to the toll worker. Now, the boyz looked the same, dressed the same, had the same cars and acted the same; They stood out from the other faces in the crowd. You couldn't miss them.

The crew from Lowellville was never concerned with the presence of local law enforcement on any of the three thousand jobs or so they planned and executed during their forty-year career. However, with knowledge that the government was now training and putting an army of new federal law people on the streets, to target groups such as theirs, people like Billy "O" had an interest in knowing when the boys from the farm were in the area. Bill was always a fair man, and insisted that everyone be compensated for their contribution to his endeavors. He never minded having one of his people personally delivering the bonuses earned by toll booth workers, who, once spotting the obvious invasion of the federal army, got word, faster than they, (The Feds) could arrive at their destinations, to Billy and others that their town was about to have "new" visitors. This timely information, yes, knowing that the feds were driving up the turnpikes from Virginia to Ohio, and not paying their tolls as they announced who the hell they were, came in handy, indeed, came in very handy, as the crew made their plans for the weekends to come.

Just for fun, Billy was driving on a state route on a clear day. He and his friend observed, after several miles, that they were being followed. Billy "O", with his sixth sense, had a hunch. He pulled into a restaurant and went inside with his pal. Sure enough, the agents following him pulled in, stopping on a dime after a rather sharp turn, to that same restaurant. Billy sat down and ordered his meal, asking the server where the men's room was located. The two other fellas from the car following him had also followed him inside. Either this was the best restaurant outside of New York City's Elaine's at the time, or he was being followed by two young Federal Agents.

While Billy "O" walked back to the men's room, he made a quick exit out the back door. He got down under his car and saw a radio signal device taped to his muffler. Billy "O" wanted to send a message to the new agents. He took the device from his vehicle and taped it to another vehicle in the lot that was the same make as his, and went back inside. He washed his hands as he came out of the men's room. Soon, both Billy "O" and his pal left the restaurant. The agents, who apparently wanted to remain undercover, waited several minutes as it where, then walked out the front door. Although they lost sight of Billy "O"'s car, they had their beeping signal still working, as they continued to follow him for miles, and miles and miles.

After about three hours or so, even the rookie agents knew something was wrong. They were following the beeper placed on the vehicle, but it was definitely not heading in the direction they had anticipated Billy was going to that day. After two hundred miles, the agents peddled the metal and pulled the car over. It took approximately thirty minutes or so for the two agents to profusely, and repeatedly, apologize and beg the forgiveness of the distinguished lady and her daughter who were occupants in the "beeping car". Billy "O", never one to laugh at the misfortune of another, knew the agents would be in for a lecture. A few years later, Billy crossed paths with the agents who tailed Mrs. John Q. Public that day, much to their professional detriment. One of the agents didn't hesitate to speak his mind. "You know, you S.O.B., you cost me six months of retraining. They sent my ass back to surveillance school in California. I owe you one!" The two men laughed as they parted company. They would, in all likelihood, meet on the battlefield of cops vs. robbers on another day. Billy had a new respect for the agent, often referring to him as a good man. They were both caught up in the same game, and they both knew it.

Chapter XXXVIII

THE MAVERICK

Many of the mob movies straight outta Hollywood often depicted scenes with "mobsters" shouting and arguing over whether someone had permission to operate in another's territory. Other such conversations, not as loud, usually ended with a gunshot and a pair of cement shoes. Billy Olive knew many of these formally "made" Mafia members. The top guys from Cleveland and Pittsburgh, which took one half each of all the action in Youngstown, knew about Billy and his crew. Yet, he was a maverick of sorts. As long as he fenced or sold his merchandise equally to the Cleveland and Pittsburgh mob, and made both of them money, Billy was free to operate. No one said a word. One long time gangster remarked "it was the damndest thing he had ever seen". Speculation regarding this phenomenon surrounding the fact that Billy Olive, the one time left-handed baseball professional prospect, while pitching no hitters and other gems in Minor league baseball, was more impressively pitching a perfect game, for several decades, in a much different game.

Billy and his crew would go out once or twice a weekend. Over the span of a year, a conservative estimate concluded that Billy "O"'s team planned and pulled off more than 100 heists a year, for at least thirty years, without every once, yes, ever once being caught in the act. Sure, he had a rumble or two, when an unexpected civilian stumbled up the scene, but that did not result in any inconvenience or botched job. They just left the area and came back later.

The local mafia families never had to worry about screw ups or foul ups, something that occurred more often than the "Dons" would prefer. When Billy "O" was in charge of the job, it was money in the bank, or out of the bank as in most cases. Billy was keen on this insight. He would often say, "The head of a family is only as good as its brain power. There are too many dumb bastards trying to be burglars or master thieves. They are way short on smarts!" As an example, Billy had to recruit one of the official members of a New York family to crew a heist at a local drug store. They were not after the drugs, but other merchandise they carried back in the day, from jewelry, clothes, Gillette razor blades and shampoo and other costly hygiene items. The most prized possession, wherever you could find them, were cigarettes. Americans loved to smoke, and Billy "O" knew it. Yet, the people of this great country would rather pay half price, than the marked up cigs in a carton put out by the tobacco big shots. Cigarettes were sold on the street as fast as they could steal them.

Billy preferred to work with a five-man crew. Some say he was superstitious, but the plain fact was that this master thief, a savant when it came to numbers and counting important data, had his game, whether it was baseball or safe cracking, down to a science. On this heist, each member of the crew had to smuggle in a nondescript empty duffle bag, to a staked out drug store. The entry that night was impeccable. All the palms had been greased, and all that was left to do was fill the duffle bags and rumble to the getaway car. As on many other occasions, it was not until they were back at the safe house, a.k.a. "The Hole in the Wall Club," owned by their sometime partner, Police Chief Michael Ciccirella, that the bags were opened and inventory of what was taken, its value on the black market, and whether any of the boys fancied something special they wanted for their wives or children, was discussed. The first three men on the heist opened duffle bags that were filled with wonderful things that a "fence" would find in a Christmas stocking. It was a great haul, so far. Yet, as the "mob guy", the one taken along as a favor, stepped up to open his duffle bag, you could see disaster coming. After all the work that was done to pull off the perfect heist of the week, the mafioso poured out the contents of his bag. As the contents taken became clear to all involved, a collective belly laugh was had. The official gangster filled his bag with nothing but cases of Listerine mouthwash! After regaining their composure, all eyes were on Billy. He could barely contain himself. "I don't know what your boss is going to say, but you better find a town where everyone has a lot of bad breath!"

It later turned out that this crew member, who belonged to a New York family, and was on the FBI's most wanted list, kept safes that he had stolen with other family members, in plain view in his basement. The serial numbers and identification numbers were still on all of the safes. If the FBI stumbled into the basement of his home, he would have gone directly to jail, and, no doubt, have become the stool pigeon of the year. Lady luck owed Billy that much.

The straw that broke the camel's back arrived when a burglar, from an out-of-state crime family, almost blew Billy's entire operation. This "gentleman" was so bad at his profession, that he was caught twice robbing the same store, and on a third attempt, fell through a hole in the ceiling, breaking his leg and calling an ambulance for assistance. At his sentencing, the presiding Judge stated, "you are the most pathetic burglar I ever had to sentence. Now beat it and don't come back to this state!" That was the last time that Billy "O" honored a made member's request to include their own. This gangster went down in history as the first guy to be fired from the local mob! Bill would often laugh when telling the stories later on, naming these leeches from the mob after one of his favorite movies, "Dumb and Dumber."

Chapter XXXIX

MR. OLIVE, YOU
HAVE CANCER

There is a certain connection today among people who have lost loved ones to cancer. There is a close bond between people who are fighting cancer. Today, there is hope for a potential cure, effective treatment and a promise for living a long and full life. Where there is hope, fear leaves the room.

Yet, it wasn't more than thirty years ago that the word 'cancer' was a body blow that could knock the best of us to the canvas. Breast cancer, brain cancer, colon cancer and more would shatter the lives of those on the opposite end of this diagnosis. For men in those days, colon cancer was a virtual death sentence. The chemo-therapies were worse than the treatment. The popular notion that the "treatment will kill you before the disease itself" held true in many cases. Some men had the option of colo-rectal surgery. Sections of the colon would be removed, all at once or over a period of time, followed by more rounds of chemotherapy. Unfortunately, with advanced colon cancer, one was only promised today, and for most of these patients at the time, with families and loved ones to support, that wasn't good enough.

Sometime in the 1980's, Billy "O" was on a roll. He was living a full life. An honored baseball player, a family man, a silent angel to some, Billy was yet operating the nearly 80-year-old family gutter and repair business, when something felt "wrong." Billy was that kind of guy who wouldn't complain of anything affecting his health, even if you gave him a million dollars. (Well, maybe not in that case.) Bill noticed, one day in his middle age plus, that he was passing blood when moving his bowels. Thanks to the internet today, much reliable information can be found on the subject of cancer. But at that point in time, Billy had not been to a doctor since he left the United States Army in 1953. Finding a doctor without having a personal medical history was an extremely difficult task. As Bill continued to experience these symptoms, he forced himself to find one.

A wonderful medical practice in a neighboring town, consisting of two brothers practicing medicine, took Billy "O" in as a patient. It was a good thing. It was a timely thing. Some would say, it was a divine thing. Billy anticipated spending only an hour or so during his appointment, but his plans for the rest of the day would have to be cancelled. "Bill, you have stage four colon cancer. It's spreading. If you don't let us take you now, and I mean now, to the surgical center downtown, you are going to die." Billy, after a few moments of reflection, quipped back to the doctor, "If you say so." The doctors at a nearby hospital performed emergency colo-rectal cancer surgery on Bill, removing 75% of his colon. Most of the staff never thought he would make it through the procedure. True to form, Bill later told one of his nurses that he didn't mind the anesthetic, as he mused, "If I am going to die, I might as well get a little rest before I go." Bill came out of the surgery, no worse for wear. He avoided the challenge of a colostomy bag, but was put on a new regime of heavy doses of chemotherapy.

Billy, on his own accord, left the hospital three or so days after the lifesaving surgery. He went home, and while never changing his lifestyle, continued with his new regime of chemo. Most people are physically drained after receiving this therapy, many require days of rest. Billy "O" had to be different, not by choice, but just because that was how he rumbled. After his scheduled routine treatments, instead of resting at home for a few days, Billy headed for the nearest diner. He made a practice of eating after every treatment, saying to inquisitors, "I feel great. I am just a little hungry. Sit down and have a bite." That was twenty-two years ago. Bill never let anyone see him sweat, not even the devil himself.

Chapter XL

FASHION BY OLIVE

"Coco Channel, Ralph Lauren, Calvin Klein, Prada." One designer after another. I often wonder why a sweater or dress with a designer label is marked up ten times compared to a garment of the same style and fit. Paying for "the label" isn't anything new. Maybe, just maybe, there is something special in the likes of these famous designers that is worth another month of your salary, or to keep that certain someone "happy", even if for a day.

The New York garment district was the start of it all in America. Taking signals from Paris, many young artists and graphic designers lay crammed in their overpriced, undersized Manhattan apartments as they did the daily grind, waiting to be discovered. The stories of famous designers are diverse, yet alike. They often earn their keep by doing any sort of task to earn a spot on the payroll of these well-known fashion giants. Many of the household designer brands began their career by sketching and doing artwork for fashion houses. Some also began in the proverbial mail room. The point is, it's unusual to rise to the top of even a local fashion market without learning the ropes, putting your time in and of course, having talent.

Calvin Klein and the likes of these superstars had to anticipate what the public wanted, and then, give it to them. Their ideas and concepts had to be unique. They had to obtain financial backing. One bad outing could cost them their career, becoming persona "non grata" in the industry. Somewhere in the rubbish of a landfill are tons of cloth, materials used in sample designs and fashion designs that just didn't make it. They are biodegrading hopefully, harmlessly filtering into the ground and back into the circle of life. Sadly, along with the piles of design failures, are buried the hopes and dreams of the designer. It is a competitive industry with many casualties of war. Among the many stars, like Calvin Klein, there is always the ones that didn't make it, the John Smith's of the world. No one has ever accused Northeast Ohio, in particular, the Youngstown, Ohio, area as being the birthplace of great fashion or design concepts. Back in those halcyon days of "branding" a name into a line of fashion ware, Youngstown and Lowellville, Ohio, were the last place you would expect to find a similar clothing brand venture.

Every year, without fail, the police chief of Lowellville, during his reign of corruption, tossed the best stag party this side of the East River in Manhattan. Chief Danatello loved women, gambling and a good party. And he would have one. The count annually was at least four hundred people in attendance. Poker games and roulette and other Vegas style gaming went on during the evening and early morning of the gala, in spite of their total illegality. The fact that the Chief of Police would sponsor and be the master of this parade, was perfectly normal in this part of the country at this time. Politicians, including mayors, councilmen, trustees, county commissioners, fellow police chiefs and even an FBI man or two, who played both sides, would never miss this annual event. In fact, it would be insulting to the Lowellville top lawman to be snubbed by one of his associate's non-attendance at his gathering.

In a way, it was very much like the academy awards held annually in Hollywood, but with roaming cows and the sound of the locomotives smashing through the town each hour. You needed a ticket or invitation to get inside to rub elbows with the people who were instrumental in giving organized crime a helping hand. Yet, due to the entourages that politicians and select corrupt businessmen brought with them, and the notoriety of the citizens of the community in attendance, women, as a rule, and the males attending the stag, had to be dressed to the nines. Most of the men attending absolutely knew that you would not be permitted inside the door entrance without wearing a beautifully cut suit, tie and jacket. That was a requirement which would not be waived for the President himself. As the attendees began to gather inside, playing no limits poker, slot machines, dice games and Texas hold 'em, an announcement would be made that dinner was being served. This was the chance for the police chief to make his grand stand, by way of a short but thankful speech, in which he assured everyone he was indeed their friend who was, and would be, always available in their time of need.

As the dinner bell rang out, the guests took their assigned seats, no names, as the chief would now hold court so to speak, admiring his friends, their power and influence, and the respect factor that came along with their attendance. At the end of the meal, the chief of law enforcement in this American town made a short speech using phrases that highlighted love of country and other mutual admiration statements. Finally, on this occasion, the mayor was compelled, after looking at the dapper crowd, to comment and praise them on their attire. Each of them, to the last, wore the latest in New York men's fashion, finely cut European suits, appropriate ties of a certain color, fitted shirts and pants with sewn in pleats. The shoes, which shine reflected off the casino lights above, revealed an elegance in their selection of Italian made leather foot coverings. The mayor, overwhelmed by these acts of respect, thanked each of them for coming as they stood "on line" as they made their exit. But he also noticed that many, if not most of the guests, had full length leather jackets on. He thought, "Life must be good, God bless this country." After a while, his assistant, Ralph D., came over and whispered to him, "Chief, what a party, and look at the style we are setting for our community. We dress like we are guests at the Whitehouse."

The mayor, crooked and corrupt as he was, was yet, not a complete idiot. Something that was floating around in the back of his mind finally was verbalized. "Yeah Ralph, our people looked great. No one could say the Italian people don't know how to dress." Ralph, the sycophant of the gala, echoed "Yeah, it all looks so classy, just wonderful. Billy "O", now he has taste!" The chief wandered to the back of the bar, where a dice game was still in progress, with a cigar lit while chomping it in his mouth. That lingering hard to track down thought, finally hit him. That son of a bitch Olive, those are "his" clothes, the "leathers" he fenced after the Kentucky warehouse job last week. The Chief ran back and grabbed Ralph, "That bastard Billy Olive!" Ralph interrupted, "But they looked great, didn't they?" "That's not the point, I had twenty percent of that action. I am going to arrest this hoodlum. Go and get the judge over there, the short guy at the craps table. He is going to sign a warrant for his arrest, now!"

The remaining guests sheepishly filed out, as Ralph took the good man to the back of the hall, reminding him he might be ruining his image. The irony of it all never escaped me. Billy "O", as it were, took no guff from anyone. The top cop was on the receiving end for once, maybe by mistake, maybe on purpose, with Billy "O", one never knew.

Chapter XLI

JOCKEYS FOR SALE

Sometimes trying to convince a genius, an ex-wife, a yankee fan or some other irrational individual that they may be wrong regarding a very important matter, is like, according to Thomas Paine, administering medicine to the dead. It doesn't work. Nothing was truer than in Billy's case. A degenerate gambler, by his own admission, and a bad one at that, Billy "O" liked to play the horses. Billy didn't like to lose; Ever. If he couldn't pick them the right way, hitting trifectas and the daily doubles only to have the race challenged, he would make sure his horses would finish "in the money". The solution was simple. When all else fails, fix the race.

In those days, during the 1950's and 60's, it was easier to find a jockey on the take, and in on a fixed race, than finding an honest horseman. The sport of Kings had come, and fallen a long way. Billy "O" would be able to fix these races in his sleep. It was almost not worth the challenge, except for the money he needed to hit the major casinos in Atlantic city. The only more financially challenged individual than a person who owned a horse, who paid enormous amounts of money required for its upkeep, was its jockey. Their short stature attracted their early discovery. They spent the first ten years of their life, starting at birth, learning how to ride horses. Their pay and living quarters were, in the best of terms, less than adequate. They lived, ate and slept with these glorious animals. Each of them, as it were, were not adverse or allergic to making a buck. When Bill honed in on a 13-1 underdog, and the arrangement was made for his favorite to come in, Billy himself, at first, was too embarrassed to collect the payout from his "winning" ticket. The term "Long Shot" actually meant just that! Not a soul in the place didn't suspect a fix. Anyone showing up to collect on a bet like this one would be sure to attract the attention of the bobbies. That caused Billy pause, if only for a second of two, as he collected his ticket and left the track for the day.

But the beauty of horse racing, and betting of course, comes in a number of flavors. People that love horses always find a way to get behind the nooks and crannies of the track, to that magical place where the horses "warm up" for the race. There, they see the horses tied to a wheel, their jockeys walking them around in a circle, keeping their legs nimble. Real horse people are able to look, watch and listen to these beautiful animals as they prepare for their majestic prance around the dirt laden track. Many times, real horse people have a sixth sense about a horse. They can tell, just by watching their favorite for a few minutes, whether the animal is in a good mood that day, how his right leg feels, whether he is tired, or lathered up, and finally, there is, like with all living things, that look in the eye of the horse. It's a glance, a personal moment between a horse and a human being. The glance is for no one else but the person who is looking. If you are not at the right distance or angle, the glance means nothing. If the sun is blocking your view, you will miss the magic. This glance, the one that tells you what he is thinking, how he feels and whether he is ready to run, is perfect, private and meant only for one person's eyes; His secret admirer.

Billy "O" loved horse races. He was either on a job, at the track or in a casino. With the beauty of the animal and competition as a background, horse racing, in particular in New Jersey, made the mob a ton of money. They controlled most of the tracks. When people placed a bet on the horse, they gave the teller money. In exchange, the teller gave the person a betting receipt. Simple enough. If their horse won, they would be paid. If it were to lose, the money stays with the house, and the house always wins. Money, like many other things, has to be placed somewhere for safe storage. The racing track at this derby was no exception. Long after the races for the day or evening were over, the money collected by the house was tucked neatly inside the four walls of a safe, located inside the office of the park. Darkness would overcome the rural setting, and the workers would leave for the night.

Billy never mixed business with pleasure, as he did at that unnamed downs that weekend. He had cased the place per his perfect plan of execution, entering the premises that evening with his crew, in such a quiet matter that no one horse with its super hearing could detect a whisk of their presence. As they performed the only surgery they knew, the safe cracked open. Its lock fell silently onto the carpeted floor below. It was payday early, as Thursday night quickly disappeared into Friday morning.

Each of the crew took their share, as was their custom, and were three counties away before the local authorities discovered the heist. Yet Billy, in a way tempting fate, and with an unknown battle royale in full swing with the demons and angels of his gambling addiction, decided to stay in town, just another night, to admire the beauty of the animals he so loved, and to bet on them. If there were ever a truer saying than "the house always wins," it was proven time and time again, at any race track in America. On Sunday night, when it was time to depart, Billy "O", riding high only hours ago, was gambling blues broke. He had given every last penny back to the house. One of his good friends later pleaded with him, "Bill, forget the horse tracks and casinos, you can't win." "You got back luck or something". Instead of wasting and risking your time and talent, just send each of your favorite places of chance a Christmas card each year, with a check enclosed in the amount you usually lose, wishing them a very merry Christmas, and apologizing that you won't be able to make it out that way this year. You would save yourself a lot of time and aggravation!

Billy laughed, and then while turning his head to the right, mumbled, "If you say so."

Chapter XLII

THE ROAD HOME AND THE THIRD VISITOR

Billy "O" was done for the day. He had what he estimated was two hundred bucks or so in his sack. Now he would exchange the scrap for cash. His routine would then take him home for the day. He put the burlap sack of his jewels over his weathered shoulder and headed toward the door. At ninety years young, that just wasn't a bad day. He was still making money, scrapping, like he did when he was a kid. Life, as he was learning, was like a circle. He was now coming back around to where it all began.

Bill began walking toward his garage door, dodging a piece of untethered falling scrap iron, admiring collectables he acquired over the years, looking at the chipped green paint on the left wall and the partially bowed ceiling to the right, thinking the entire time that he needed to hurry to the scrap yard before it closed. The mid-afternoon wind whistled through, clanging and clinging things hanging on walls at times thought to be a voice trying to be heard. He brushed it off, after looking over his shoulder. He focused on the getaway path, toward the door. Bill stepped through the peeled paint falling off the wedged front door, pushing it outward, to make his exit as he had done a thousand and one times before. He was eager to return home and have his lunch and make a call to a friend, thus the reason for the extra push. To Billy "O"'s surprise, the door was not cooperating. At ninety years old, he had faced worse. Billy now, out of reflex, relied on his muscle memory. Every athlete has such a gift. The body ages but the mind never forgets. William George Olive leaned into it. The jammed door burst open, and as he was beginning his walk through, he heard the sound of the train and the thrill of his whistle. But the savant with the knack for numbers, knew something was amiss. The timing was off. A five o'clock train in the mid-afternoon? Maybe his mind was indeed finally giving in.

The mighty Mahoning rushes underneath the iron rusted bridge, holding secrets since 1820 of tales and union missions, runs for steel, a witness to all things that ever occurred in Lowellville; Its iron, bent and stretched as it arcs over the waters, acting as a protective hood for the rush of the muddy, mighty Mahoning, was always a magnificent display. The brick streets, the bridge, the river that never sleeps and the tracks, always the tracks which are located at the intersection of fortune and destiny, complete the great work of art that represented this village. The hazy street lamps shed low light into the nights guiding men and women on secret rendezvous, and ghosts and spirits and angels, all drawn, to the point; The rails and the crossing wooden guards, able centurions, soldiering on after many years of wind and decay, still announcing the arrival of steel on wheels. The energy of that universe met at a single point on this day, at a single instant, the mojo of it all conjured up by the watchman of the village, Pop Shraum. The moving of the trains, the tracks giving them flight, the strident, mighty river, the haze, the sunset, whistles, the rustling of the bushes respecting not time or fate, were all about to witness something of another dimension.

Pops Shraum, George Mathew Shraum, was kneeling next to the tracks. He had passed some seventy-five years ago. His soul was shackled and spiritually bound to that location, waiting to be released by some words or gesture, or answers to questions he had pondered for those seventy-five years. He was seeking privilege to leave and find his new, final peace. But first, there had to be a reckoning, a closing of that chapter in time.

William George Olive is ninety years old. He is alive. The meeting at that location and at that exact time and place happened on two occasions in the history of time; At this moment, in one form or another, and seventy-five years ago when young Bill was searching for George Shraum, the father of his father, to come home for dinner.

Billy "O" begins approaching his grandfather. With each step, the years peeled off, until he stood over his grandfather's spirit. He was fifteen again, when he ended his pace, and Pop Shraum was there where he saw him.

"Billy, I knew you would come back for me. Is it time to get your dad and call it a day?"

"Pops, I am ninety years old. We lost you..a long time ago."

"What the heck are you talking about? You've been spending too much time chasing those critters'...you get lost in those woods back up there and you go stir crazy, lose your young mind." "We better get going, your mom's waiting."

"Mom is gone Pops, so is Popa Dominic, your son, my father, ..I am sorry for both of us".

"How could....am I in a dream?"

"No. I am here, Papa."

"I have been waiting for you seventy-five years." "I remember now."

"Pops, I would walk through hell to be there, have another chance to save you."

"I know son…but it doesn't work that way."

"I couldn't wait any longer. They said you were killed by that train pops. I saw you lying there, you couldn't move, pops! I ran. I didn't know what to do. I was scared. I was just a boy."

"There was nothing you could do son. Things happen. I miss you Billy, and your father too."

"Things happen. But you came back. I called you".

"I watched you Bill, from here, sitting, for nearly eighty years, I think. But I saw everything you did."

The sunset lit up the iron rails holding down the magic railroad tracks. The town was ready for sleep.

"I got that contract with the professional baseball team."

"I know bill. I am sorry how it turned out."

"You mean the money?"

"No, that you didn't make your dream come true."

"I was eighteen pops, I didn't know what I wanted."

"I prayed for you when you were in Korea. So much death Billy, and sitting here, by these tracks, listening to the bells, rung each time a death.. I felt it all. My god Bill, the inhumanity."

"You almost died on that ship, going over."

"I thought I did."

"Did you think I was really going to let that happen?"

"Can you believe they made me an M.P.?"

"Yes, I can, you were brought up good."

"I wept for everyone, for every soul given to that war, but I don't know why, and can't remember all the details. It's like I was there, but I was here too, at the same time....but I came back tonight to see you, to talk with you."

"It tried to help some of the people."

"You married before you left."

"But I met someone over there Pops...I was far away from home."

"I know, Bill. But she was badly hurt by a bomb, and disappeared at the end of the war." "I don't know what happened to her after that. She really loved you, Bill."

"These tracks are kind of funny. I think I am still in this one place, but with the magic of the railroad...you can go anywhere, and come back again."

"Sit down son."

"Are you disappointed in me?"

"You were never brought up to steal."

"We were proud of you Billy."

"I was here the night young Bill Jr. passed.... I felt your heart break. But I couldn't come to you."

"I feel like I never left this place Pops, but I know that isn't true.

"But you came back home, you took back Olive and watched over young Bill...to the end."

"I want to say I am sorry for what I did...but I am not...I chose that life..."

"Billy, if saying your sorry, would it change what you did?

"No, it happened...I lived like a thief."

"So, what are you looking for Bill? Redemption, forgiveness?"

"I am not sure Pops." "Maybe nothing."

"That's not true Bill, you walked out that door this morning. You could have sat back down when the door jammed, but you fought back. You used every ounce of strength to come here."

"I don't know if I had a choice."

"We always have a choice. It's the rule."

"It's what we do at the end, when we have a choice to look back, to confirm what we have done wrong... or reject it."

"That door didn't jam by itself. You could have stopped and waited for help, but you didn't, you knew it was the only way back, to here." You were looking for something else." " Examine your soul, seek the truth and you will find it."

Chapter XLIII

THE CONFESSION

B illy Olive slowly walked up the five steps or so leading from the sidewalk to the doors of the glistening stone cathedral-where the pavement of Wood and Queisner Streets intersected. He was back where it all had begun. He didn't need anyone's help, walking with his now forward leaning elongated gait, each step a potential catastrophe, his height an inch or so less by time, his shoulder leaning to one side. As the ninety year old that he was, Billy wondered if he had the strength to open the heavy metal doors that provided passage into the house of God. It was a Saturday afternoon, when confessions were heard by the local priest, and there were not many people present to assist him. He thought of turning and walking back down the steps, but feared, in his advanced age, tumbling down them and meeting his death before he could breach the doors leading to his possible penance. He had entered many places over the years, without invitation, but now, there was a presence inside beckoning him to enter.

His somewhat dark, hollowed out eyes gazed upon the grand brass designs on the church door. He thought, briefly, how beautiful it looked. As he took a breath of air, and braced himself on his right leg, as when he was a pitching sensation, his body remembered how to move as he grasped the door leading to the place of his salvation. The wind saw it fit not to be harsh against the brass that day, lest he be denied entrance by the elements.

The door, from an inside perspective, opened slowly, and the thin aperture allowed for a piercing beam of sunlight to enter the darkness of its decor. From the cross, one could, and one may have looked down, in all his pain, and witnessed his young child finally coming back to his hallowed home in this town of souls. The door opened a slight bit more. Young Bill felt the late arriving wind, now pushing him into the cathedral, taking his breath away for only an instant, as he pushed his body through the entrance and into the holy sanctuary. Billy moved his head from side to side, taking in the beauty of it all. His mind began to fill with fleeting thoughts imprinted in younger days, of the awesome beauty and reverence displayed by the marble pillars and stained glass windows, which reflected the sunlight in ways that were, as no other word would suffice, angelic. The church, in all its silent splendor, revealed images of Mother Mary embedded into the blinding ceiling, above the far away altar, as statues of saints stood like centurions on the side aisles. Walking down the aisle, to William, seemed now, in some peculiar way, like an out of body experience. He looked up briefly to the crucifix, suspended high above the altar by a series of wires attached to the immaculate ceiling above. For the first time in seventy-five years, William Olive, in less than an instant and more than an eternity, felt an awesome, totally overpowering, all consuming sense of peace. He thought, "Maybe, I am finally home."

Billy "O" took the walk down the center aisle toward the altar, at times holding onto the side of pews, to balance himself. He noticed an elderly lady, rosary in hand, on the right side of him. The majesty of the ornate silver chalice, gold crucifix, chandeliers hanging from the ceiling, stations of the cross carved into wood along the side of the venue, were almost too much to wrap his soul around. These sensations heightened his "dulled with time" senses. The thickness of this force of purity, first stripped Billy of his false pride, then lifted him to heights of a renewed humility. Billy, for a short time, felt a presence, that power of something certain.

The quiet solitude the venerated site provided him also provided safe sanctuary, peace and protection from the world existing outside of the brass doors. It was as if he stepped out of time and into a place that operated under different rules. He sensed, unmistakingly, the uncorrupted spirit of a young boy who was there before the carnal pleasures of life hollowed and corroded his body, spirit and mind. He was in a place of renewal, the place of second chances. He placed his aging frame into the pew, sitting first, then managing to kneel. He held fast to the wooden rail in front of him, so as not to sway. It had been awhile.

Bill had promised Pops George Matthew Shraum, in his vision, that he would indeed go to the local church for confession. Both men had, initially, personal motives for the act. William had always obeyed his elders, and whether he was twelve years old or ninety, he respected Pop's request. Now, the true final confession, which was seventy-five years in the making, was only steps away. Bill took a moment to gather his senses, harnessing those peaceful feelings, looking again to the cross above the altar. For some apparently unknown reason, he had been drawn toward the front row. He half smiled in resignation as he thought he would not be able to walk the long path of stone, across the slippery marble floor of the church, to arrive at the confessional station. When realizing his plight, William, for the first time, and after all of the madness in his life, began to panic. He then did something he hadn't done since the death of his son Bill Jr.; he prayed.

Churches, like casinos, have no clocks on the wall. People attending Sunday services, for many reasons, fail to look at their watches when there, maybe out of respect or the fear of being seen as someone looking for a quick exit. But Bill, without a watch and nowhere to be, was at ease, waiting for events to play out, trusting that a gift would come to him. Out of the corner of his eye, Billy "O" began picking up shadowy images, gliding up and down the dark side aisles of the church, where the statues of saints lined the walls. He imagined dark hoods whispering in soft, secret voices, making beautiful, but quiet song, chanting as if in a 14th century monastery. The spiritual atmosphere, whether real or imagined by his less than perfect elderly mind, overwhelmed Billy Olive. Suddenly, in an instant, one of the figures placed his hand on Bill's right shoulder, startling him. The unannounced man knelt next to Bill. "In the name of the Father, and of the Son, and of the Holy Spirit. "I am Father Dominic, William. I am here to take your confession."

Some men of the cloth leave the sanctuary of the confessional booth to accommodate the elders, and Father Dominic was one. After regaining his exposure, Bill whispered, as an automatic behavior, although the church was empty save for the one rosary penitent, "Father, I made a promise to come here and make my confession. I haven't been here since I was a boy, but I hope you won't hold that against me." The vicar of Christ looked upon the cross, turning his head, " I don't think he will hold it against you. Tell me Billy, what sins have you come to confess."

For the next two hours, the two men talked in the presence of God. Bill had purged himself of all the things he had done, his violation of and commandments. " I have neglected my wife and son, and ruined my family's name. People judge me harshly now. All of my friends are gone. I don't want to be judged or remembered like this. I know it's too late for me."

"If what you seek is forgiveness of your sins, the man on the cross has that power. God through his son, Jesus Christ, has the power to forgive sins. Ask for his forgiveness, and it will be given." Bill interrupted. "But the people…" "William, His power is universal, and it commands the souls of all purified men and women on earth. The bible says if God has forgiven you, no man has the power to judge you, lest he look at himself."

Billy remembered those bible verses from his young catechism days. At a young age, William thought they were just empty words, stories, but now felt the graveness of it all. He knew a power greater than himself, an almighty singular presence, was living inside him.

Bill then sent a private prayer and confession directly to God. As the time for Bill to leave had arrived, he stood, without aid, upon his feet. He began to walk out of the sanctuary of miracles. Billy Olive was forgiven of his sins. More importantly, he felt forgiveness. Pop Shraum was right. Bill felt total peace. He wanted to tell the first person he saw about his overwhelming experience. The elderly lady, with Rosary in hand, after all this time, was still praying a few rows of pews behind Bill. " Mam, I apologize, but could you tell me the name of the priest who took my confession. It's very important; The one that stood by me, just a few rows in front of you." " I must not have been paying close attention. Forgive me. I have been in prayer all day."

Billy seemed puzzled, "But he was here." (Bill, pointing to the location of his redemption). "I think his name was Father Dominic." The woman looked into Bill's glorified eyes. "I am sorry, I didn't see anyone. The Church, this Church, has no Father Dominic." Bill, puzzled, "But I was with him all day." "You're Billy Olive, we went to school together! I have to admit I was surprised when you came in, I mean,..the important thing is that you came." "I watched you. You knelt for only a few minutes and walked around for some time." " You only now came to me, on the way out. God bless you Billy." "The love of God is real, his power to forgive anyone, is absolute."

Billy thought he had the onset of dementia, or that he had another vivid dream, as when Bunnie and Pinky came to him. Like many times before, he smiled and shrugged his shoulders. "If you say so."

Billy walked down the aisle, looking up to the organist's balcony, as he blessed himself with holy water. He opened the doors to the last of the sunlight, which caused a tear to come to his eye. It needed to be wiped away. By instinct, he reached into his pocket for a hand-kerchief. His left hand, the one made of jelly, felt a cloth. As Willaim pulled it out from his left pocket, it was saturated, soaked, as if he had used it to wash his face or dry his tears. It had the symbol of the cross on it; But he never carried with him anything of the sort. Billy saw the security guard heading over to lock the Church doors. "What about the older lady, she is finishing her rosary, don't lock her in." "There is no one there, sir, you were the only one that came here today."

William Olive began the slow walk back to his senior citizen apartment. He had to cross over the town's mystical railroad tracks, something he had done many times before during his long, long life, near the mighty Mahoning. But this time he felt a rock had been lifted from this shoulder. He didn't bother questioning his state of mind. The point was that he fulfilled the promise he made to Pop Shraum, and as usual, Pops was right. As Bill heard the second locomotive approaching on the side track, with the bells and whistles chiming simultaneously with those in the cathedral across the street, he looked back out of sheer reflex, after all these years, to see if Pops Shraum was there. But the heartbreaking events of that fateful day, some seventy five years ago, were finally gone from his mind. As he walked up the green hills on the summer solstice, he still, in his heart of hearts, could have sworn he heard whispers, or maybe it was just the evening wind, carrying a message of salvation; "Welcome home Billy Olive; Welcome home."

Epilogue

illiam Olive is ninety years old. He lives in Lowellville, Ohio, near his sister Pinky and close to the town's cemetery which holds all of his family in its grounds. He doesn't expect to be there anytime soon. He has good deeds to do, and is working on a perfect season of miracles.

And the bridge stood guard over the rushing river,

as the mystical tracks kept their secrets hidden,

And all of their children were finally at rest

In a place once forbidden.

It was the hottest day of the year.

END

Made in the USA
Middletown, DE
22 July 2020